SHOES

the ultimate accessory

SHOES

the ultimate accessory

Tessa
Paul

CHARTWELL
BOOKS, INC.

This edition published in 2010 by

CHARTWELL BOOKS, INC.
A Division of
BOOK SALES, INC.
276 Fifth Avenue Suite 206
New York, New York 10001
USA

ISBN 13: 978-0-7858-2591-3
ISBN 10: 0-7858-2591-6

Produced for Compendium Publishing Ltd by:
Editorial Developments
Edgmond
Shropshire
England.

Design by: Chensie Chen

Printed in China

SHOES
CONTENTS

6 - 11   **Introduction**

12 - 43   **Story of the Shoe**

44 – 69   **1920s Dancing Shoes**

50 – 51 Seymour Troy
58 – 59 Pietro Yantorny
64 – 65 François Pinet

70 – 95   **1930s Glamour and Democracy**

76 – 77 André Perugia
84 – 85 Adidas
90 – 91 Salvatore Ferragamo

96 – 119   **1940s Austerity and Invention**

100 – 101 David Evins
108 – 109 Bata
114 – 115 Saks 5th Avenue

120 – 145   **1950s Changing Directions**

126 – 127 The Herbert Levine Company
134 – 135 Capezio
140 – 141 Massaro

146 – 171   **1960s Loafers and Liberation**

152 – 153 Bruno Magli
160 – 161 Walter Steiger
166 – 167 H&R Rayne

172 – 197   **1970s Symbolic Footwear**

178 – 179 Terry de Havilland
186 – 187 Rossetti Fratelli
192 – 193 R Griggs

198 – 223   **1980s Power Style**

204 – 205 Charles Jourdan
212 – 213 Andrea Pfister
218 – 219 Nike

224 – 249   **1990s Glamour and Status**

230 – 231 Manolo Blahnik
238 – 239 Jimmy Choo
244 – 245 Clarks

250 – 299   **2000s Dreams and Delusions**

262 – 263 Christian Louboutin
276 – 277 Bally
290 – 291 Robert Clergerie

300 – 307   **Novelty Shoes Fanciful Footwear**

302 – 303 Vivienne Westwood
306 – 307 Thea Cadabra

308 – 317   **How a shoe is made –**
A visit to the Cordwainers' College, London, England

318 – 319   **Index/Bibliography**

320   **Acknowledgements**

SHOES
INTRODUCTION

Shoes tell a fascinating history, one that reveals changes in politics, culture, and technology. This book follows that story, and in doing so, charts the liberation of western women in the twentieth century.

The first shoes were made, we must suppose, to meet necessity. Feet need to be protected from the stony, thorn-strewn earth, or shielded from cold and rain. But there is another story, and it is about the eroticism of the female foot. From the earliest times, there has been an urge within shoemakers to decorate and beautify women's feet with delectable footwear.

This book tracks the story of women's shoes and the seemingly radical direction it took in the twentieth century. Modern footwear technology produces light, comfortable, athletic footwear, yet the erotic allure of feet in high heels and encased in feathers, sequins, and bows remains the sublime purpose of women's shoes. What woman could resist the man who murmurs, "I'll take a look at your slippers. I love them as much as I do you."

LEFT: It looks as if strips of textile have been twisted to make these delectable sandals, but the appearance is disingenuous. Sophisticated computer calculations have helped devise the twisting straps and ensured that the shoes are structured to hold the feet without slipping. Modern technology has allowed the realization of a huge array of footwear design.

It is true that, for many centuries, rich men wore shoes adorned with buckles and bows, announcing the status, wealth, and importance of the wearer. Meanwhile, women's feet were hidden under long skirts and without doubt, this secrecy added to the erotic value of the female foot. Even in ancient times, women's sandals were poured with gold, or studded with jewels, evidence that women have always yearned for wonderful shoes, the kind of shoes that promise allure, shoes that promise adventure and romance. Modern American women own, on average, thirty pairs of shoes, further proof that shoes are more than merely a necessity.

There are shoes shaped to elevate the foot, making walking difficult. Some feet have been deliberately crippled to keep them small and so difficult to use. "Perhaps women were once so dangerous they had to have their feet bound," wrote Maxine Hong Kingston, and it is interesting to observe that as liberated western women of the twentieth century grew more and more powerful, so they were persuaded to wear extremely high shoes, making it impossible to move with a free, loose stride. But liberated women are also athletes, mountaineers, and sailors, and for them the shoemakers have developed scientifically designed, lightweight shoes to enable fast, nimble movement.

RIGHT: It is difficult to create designs without reference to historical sources. The banded straps and interesting spaces of these shoes hark back to an Edwardian fashion, the barrette, that had similar bands, often rising to mid-calf. In the 1940s, the great Ferragamo introduced the platform shoe, but in the modern variation, it slants inwards from the toe, making movement in the high-heeled shoe easier for the wearer.

Because, although for centuries, shoes were embroidered, beribboned, and bejeweled, the technology of our times has seen the development of ergonomics and pliable, yet durable, materials and this progress has had a profound effect on shoe manufacture. All kinds of designs and structures—once undreamt of—have been made possible. Now, there are shoes to suit every need, from the woman athlete to the foot fetishist.

Shoes have always been an important statement of wealth but, in modern times, they indicate also taste and style, regardless of financial status. On every high street, any woman can find the elegant, the conventional, the bizarre, the sporty, the frivolous, the sexy—whatever suits, it will be available easily and at no great expense. And women shop for fabulous shoes with hope in their heart: the great designer, Roger Vivier summed it up when he said, "To wear dreams on one's feet is to begin to give reality to one's dreams."

LEFT: Some shoes are simply irresistible. Look at the response to this sandal of pale cream, cut to reveal the naked arch and toes, with a naughty little shield on the heel.

STORY OF THE
SHOE

In the twentieth century, when sporting events became global, western athletes were astonished to meet African long distance runners who ran barefoot. Yet, for centuries, many peoples across the African continent never bothered with shoes. The great Zulu military leader, Chaka, made his warriors dance barefoot on fields of thorn so the soles of their feet became tough enough to withstand the rough local terrain.

In other parts of the world, people were not quite so resilient. The ancient civilizations of the Middle East contrived simple soles held to the foot with thongs, and this footwear did not alter for a very long time. Of course, details of the basic flip-flop design changed: thongs and loops were elaborated but essentially, the Ancients—the Persians, the Egyptians, the Greeks, and the Romans—wore sandals.

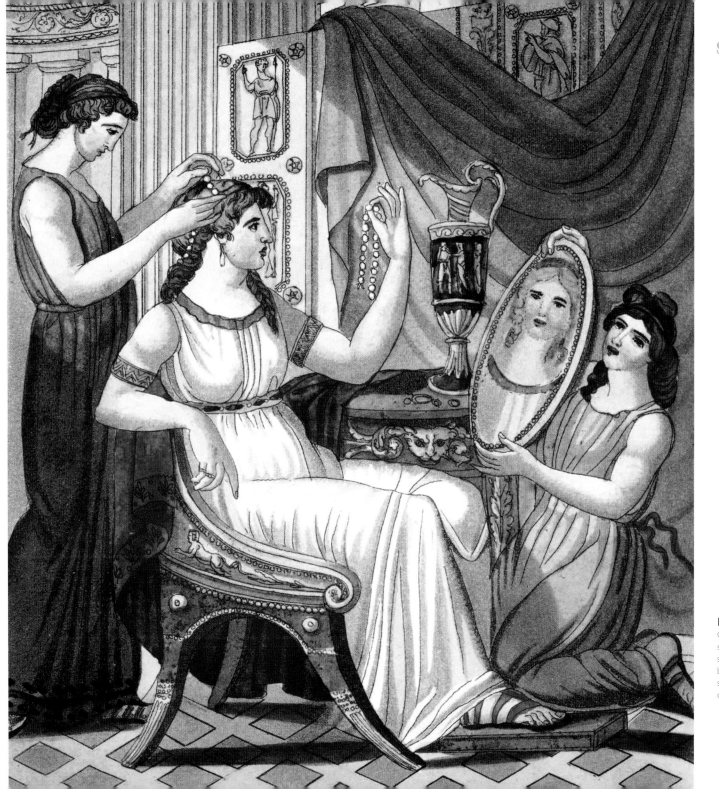

The Greeks and Romans used leather soles and thongs. The Egyptians fashioned woven Palmyra leaves, while the Indians carved soles from wood with a toe-knob round which the wearer clutched their toes to hold the sandals while walking. Rich Roman ladies had soles of gold, and Indians covered theirs with silver. On the upper face of the sole Romans and Egyptians would draw the face of an enemy so, symbolically, they could grind the hated one underfoot. Perhaps this association of the shoe as a tool of fury lingers in the Middle Eastern custom of throwing shoes as a gesture of insult.

BELOW: This sandal, one of a pair, is woven from plant fiber (papyrus and rush) and is probably New Kingdom, Eighteenth dynasty or later—after 1,500 BC. It is cleverly constructed, having a frame of curved reeds to hold the woven sole. Probably, the maker drew the shape of the foot in the sand or on clay, and used the resulting diagram to form the frame and weave a sole that fitted the wearer.

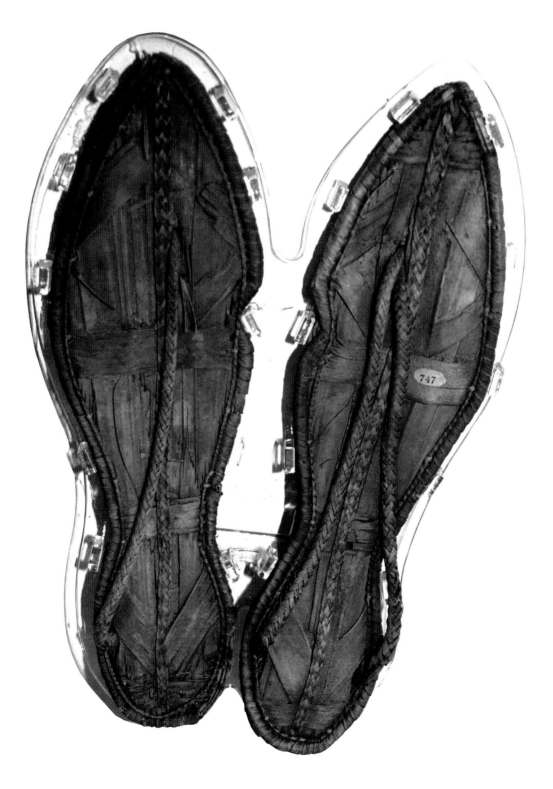

There are archaeological discoveries of other early footwear. Evidence has been found of boots shaped from a piece of leather bound with leather thongs, and of moccasins, a foot-bag seamed at the toe and the heel but, for centuries, the use of sandals was widespread among the men and women of the Middle East. This tradition was broken by a decree from the Christian Byzantine Empire based in the holy city of Constantinople (now Istanbul). Following the teachings of the third century saint, Clement of Alexandria, religious leaders announced it was immodest for women to expose their toes.

LEFT: A pair of sandals of the Roman period, possibly circa 200 AD, made from plant fiber (papyrus and rush). These are preserved in the Durham University Oriental Museum, Durham, England and are of the most basic and simple footwear design. Kept in a plastic surround to keep their shape, they are what we now call a flip-flop.

ABOVE: This is a single, right, dark leather ankle shoe, with a straight side seam and strap fastening. It dates from the fourteenth century.

BELOW: For centuries, wooden clogs were common footwear across Northern Europe. Like this example, clogs were carved from one piece of wood. Styles differed enormously, from the plain to this low-heeled version that is cut high at the front and low at back then decorated with mock side laces.

Cordwainers, the shoe makers, had to re-think their product, and developed turnshoes. These were made by wrapping leather inside out, seaming it on the inner arch, then attaching it to the sole, before the leather was turned right side out. Slowly, the combination of a sole and a leather covering was realized, creating the shoe. But well made footwear remained exclusive to the rich. During inclement weather, the poor tied cloths to their legs then bound their sandals over their stockings or, as in Northern Europe, wore clogs. These were carved entirely of wood, or had thick wooden soles with a section of leather wrapped over the toe area and nailed to the wood.

It was only in the fourteenth century that foot measurements were standardized. Cordwainers prepared shoes of various sizes but the shoes were "straight," meaning each shoe could fit either foot. These ready-made shoes were sold at the great fairs held so frequently in medieval times.

For centuries, shoes for both sexes were flat-soled and had almond shaped toes. However, in the fourteenth century, men's clothing showed off the leg and dandies took to shuffling about in pointy shoes. The toes became so ridiculously long, a papal bull in 1468 tried to banish the style. (The shoes were called pikes in England because they resembled the pointed "snout" of the freshwater pike fish.)

By the sixteenth century, cordwainers had developed the welted shoe. With this a second sole was placed over the sole, and the welt (a strip of leather) was fitted between the edges of the two soles. An insole was placed on the bottom fitting. The shoe body, or upper, was stitched and later riveted through the layers of insole, bottom fitting, welt, and sole. The upper was seamed at the heel. This construction remains the blueprint for all modern shoes.

BELOW: This is a turn shoe, in which the upper has been stitched to the sole, then turned inside out. This method of construction was used for over a thousand years, but by the sixteenth century, European cordwainers had abandoned it in favor of the hardier welted shoe.

LEFT: In the late eighteenth century, men rather than women showed off their elegant shoes. London was besieged by fashionable young men, known as "dandies" whose ridiculous collars, corseted waists, and long, pointed shoes were the delight of contemporary cartoonists and satirists.

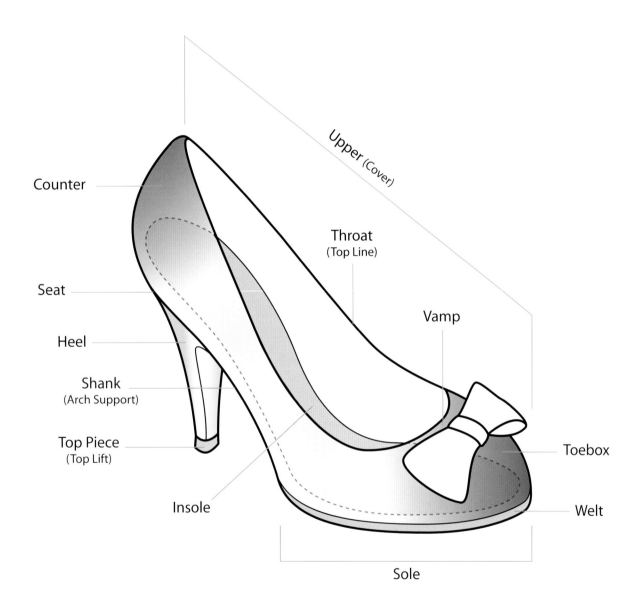

Counter

Seat

Heel

Shank
(Arch Support)

Top Piece
(Top Lift)

Insole

Upper (Cover)

Throat
(Top Line)

Vamp

Toebox

Welt

Sole

There are about a hundred operations involved in making a shoe. The shoe has an "anatomy": the throat is the edge of the shoe and the shank defines the area balancing the arch and ball of the foot. Furthermore, a shoe has a heel breast and a toe box. The "last" is a replica of the foot—traditionally, carved from wood, but nowadays it is generally molded plastic. A last is required for every size and style of shoe, and also, different lasts are required for men and women. The cordwainers, working usually in family groups, divided their skills as last makers, cutters, stitchers, and shapers; women often did the final stitching.

LEFT: The shoe has a complex design and, over the centuries, its many parts have acquired names. This diagram describes the basic components.

LEFT: Cordwainers experimented with designs to cope with bad weather and terrain. These stilted sandals were worn by women of the Ottoman Empire to protect their feet from the dust of the streets and the wet floors of the public baths. Of course, some shoemakers moved beyond the sensible and made heels so high that walking itself became difficult. Venetian chopines probably started as protection against the mud and puddles of Venice but became extravagantly high and thus, a fashion of absurdity.

LEFT: It is believed high heels first appeared in Europe at the French court after the brother of Louis XIV, tired of jeers about his short stature, ordered heels on his shoes. They soon became the rage. This pair, dated from around 1670, has a short latchet closure with a cord, dyed to match the shoe, threaded through one pair of eyes (holes).

Renaissance Italy, rich and artistic, set the fashion for Europe. Pale leather covers, slashed to show a colored lining were popular. High heels made of wood became voguish and a travelogue of 1611 recorded the chopines worn by Venetian women. These platform mules, some as high as two feet, forced the wearer to have servants support her when she walked out. To be fair, this fashion was worn by only the most foolhardy of females, but chopines are remembered as a style oddity.

Instead, slap shoes became the thing. Designed to prevent heels sinking in muddy streets, the shoe was fitted over a flat sole. Generally, this sole was attached to the shoe only at the toe, creating a slapping sound with each footfall: (hence the name.) Many have survived, probably because they weren't worn very often. A slap sole may have coped with mud but hardly made for easy walking.

LEFT: One solution to the hazards of walking in mud was the slap shoe. This elegant white kid, heeled shoe has an extra sole attached to the toe of the shoe sole, and this addition was meant to prevent the wearer from sinking into mud.

Low-heeled mules, or pantoufles, extravagantly decorated or made of colored brocade, were worn indoors. They became associated with the boudoir, and even now, in the United States, mules, adorned with marabou, or stork feathers, retain high sales as bedroom wear. Inevitably, the mule acquired an erotic aura and the marabou mule is sexy showing, as it does, the naked foot resting on a high heel, the toes partially hidden by a fluffy feathered covering.

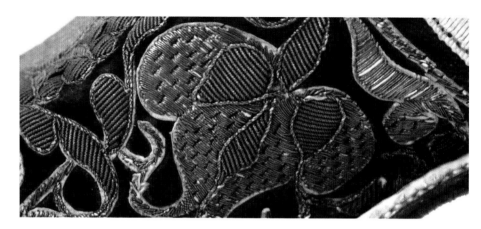

RIGHT: The deep wine-colored velvet textile has been embroidered in intricately worked threads of silvers and golds. The entwined plant forms may have been influenced by designs introduced from the Ottoman Empire.

BELOW: The upward curving toe seems to indicate an Ottoman influence, but the waisted heel and cover patterning confirm a European design. The embroidery has the free lines familiar in the West. The latchet is made for a buckle closure.

BELOW: Nicely made and decorative, these clog overshoes were made to fit over this particular pair of shoes. The fabric used on the overshoes has been matched to the shoes, and they are fastened with an elaborate little bow.

ABOVE: This brocaded shoe has a closure designed for a buckle. The high heels are painted red, a practise first demanded by a French king but which soon became the fashion of high society in the seventeenth century.

BELOW: This is a clog overshoe and seems a good solution to the problem of protecting shoes when worn outdoors. A quasi-shoe is tied over the proper shoe, thus ensuring the sole of the shoe, if not the cover, is shielded from mud and muck.

In Europe, heels were widely worn after Louis XIV (1660–1715) came to power in France. He adored thick heels and buckles but women liked slender heels, pointed toes, and ribbons to tie their shoes. Buckles caught on their hemlines, they said. (For some eccentric reason, Louis commanded all heels be painted red.) Ladies' shoes of the later eighteenth century reflected the prevailing Baroque style, and were piled high with bows, silk flowers, and beads.

LEFT: In the eighteenth century, the world of high society preferred buckles rather than ribbons as shoe closures. This selection of buckles reveals that this is a fashion that employs not only cordwainers but many different craftsmen—ceramicists, metal workers, and jewelers. The first buckle on the left is painted ceramic, while the others are worked metals, or decorated with beads and gems.

Women on country estates protected their sturdy shoes from mud with an overshoe of wood or cork soles that was strapped onto the shoe, the whole supported by an iron ring. Known as pattens, they were found in England and across northern Europe.

LEFT: The heels on these mid-eighteenth century shoes are thick but curved with a waist. The cover is embroidered and the latchets are made to fit a buckle. The needlework on the heel is frayed, showing signs of constant wear.

RIGHT: This pretty shoe with a low heel was made, perhaps, for a young wearer. The cover is embroidered silk, but the latchets are not decorated because they will be adorned with a buckle. The shoe comes from the late eighteenth century.

Even countrywomen succumbed to the cute curved heels worn by the French court of Louis XV (1710–1774): these heels are still called Louis heels. Hemlines were lifted, causing women's shoes to assume a special significance. They were decorated with huge, glittering buckles often transferred from one pair of shoes to another.

Shoes became a deliberate, even offensive statement of wealth. The French Revolution (1789) brought a halt to such showy displays. The majority of people now clumped about in shoes of plain design and crude leather, and these people were in a cruel mood, hostile towards the rich and their luxury possessions.

BELOW: After the French Revolution, embroidered shoes were seen as ostentatious, and cordwainers turned to less expensive methods of decoration. For instance, this pink shoe has been roller-printed with tiny gold scales. The shoe is further embellished with a narrow, tightly frilled fringe on the vamp.

ABOVE: The vamp of this flat pump shows cut leather with a pale gold inlay, a quiet decoration that suited the mood for a modest, simple appearance, so fashionable at the turn of the nineteenth century.

The nineteenth century opened to a post-revolutionary mood and everyone wanted to show approval of the new social equality. Imitating the style of democratic Ancient Greece, women's dresses were narrow and toga-like—a style known ironically as "Empire" dress. They were worn with low-heeled or flat shoes. Sandals were considered immodest, but flat shoes were made with cut-outs, to further copy the Greeks.

Paved streets appeared at the beginning of the nineteenth century and wealthy women chose not to be carried about in a sedan chair but to walk. The habit became faddish and was called "pedestrianism," so fashionable ladies wore foothold galoshes to protect their flimsy footwear. The woman fitted her shoe into a covered toe, while at the heel end of the galoshes was a ring to hook over the heel of the shoe. The leather of outdoor shoes was considerably improved by waterproof japanning. This involved painting the leather with several coats of varnish and oil.

LEFT: This style of flat pump, with long ribbons that lace up the leg, was known as the sandal slipper. Sandals that revealed the toes were considered shocking, so these strappy simple shoes were a pretty substitute, as well as being economical. The flat sole was cheap to make and could be worn on either foot and, apparently, these qualities encouraged women to purchase more than one pair. The sandal slipper was popular in the 1830s.

ABOVE: The long, narrow vamp and a blunt toe combine to make comfortable indoor footwear. But the beautiful embroidered decoration takes this mule from the cosy into the realms of glamorous boudoir slippers.

LEFT: It is a pity the designer of this mule is anonymous, he deserves better. The line of the cover is cut to echo the curve of the heel and sole, giving the mule a graceful profile. Low-heeled mules had once been common wear throughout Europe but as heels got higher, the shoes were confined to house wear. This mule is low-heeled and easy to wear in most environments, but perhaps too beautiful to risk in dust or mud.

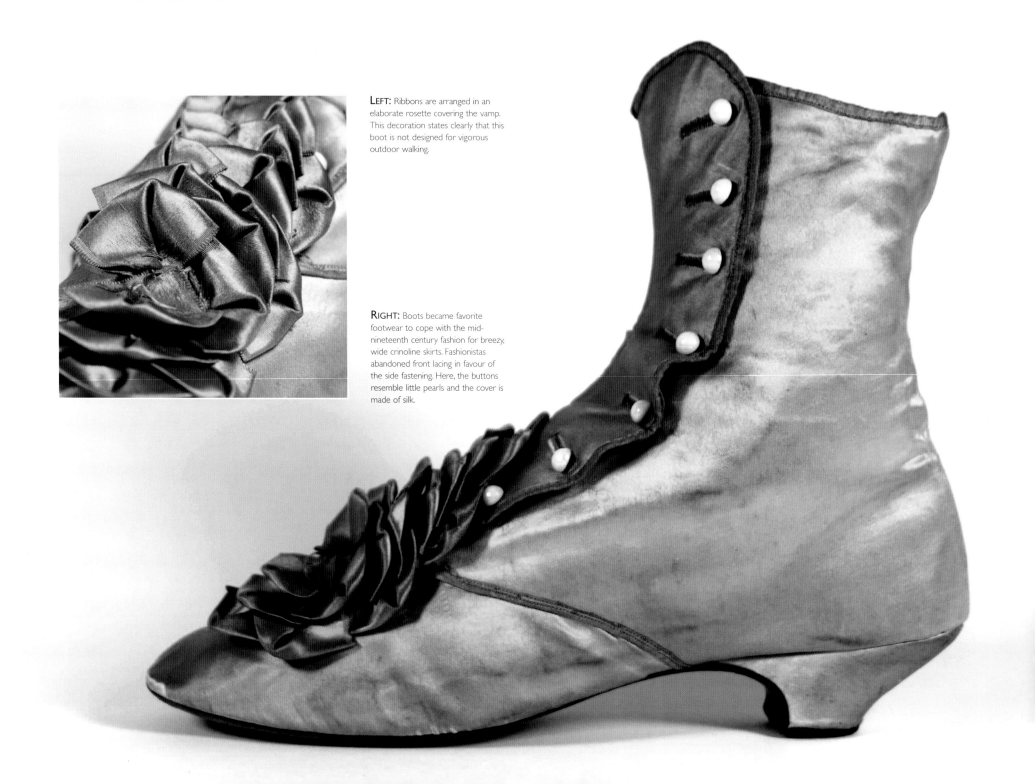

LEFT: Ribbons are arranged in an elaborate rosette covering the vamp. This decoration states clearly that this boot is not designed for vigorous outdoor walking.

RIGHT: Boots became favorite footwear to cope with the mid-nineteenth century fashion for breezy, wide crinoline skirts. Fashionistas abandoned front lacing in favour of the side fastening. Here, the buttons resemble little pearls and the cover is made of silk.

By the 1860s, huge crinoline skirts had returned, accompanied by ankle boots with button closures or front-lacings. The laced style was known as the Balmoral boot and Queen Victoria observed that, when wearing Balmorals, a "high-born lady may . . . take a good walk with pleasure and safety." Even with the invention of elastic gussets on boots, the laced boot did not lose its appeal. Victorian gentlemen seemed to enjoy the duty of loosening the laces.

LEFT: Lining each side of the front lacing, braid has been arranged to copy frog fastenings, then extended into a fantasy of loops and whirls to decorate the vamp and the back of the boot. The patterning makes a feminine interpretation of the grandiose military wear of the Victorian Age, although it's hard to believe this delicious pair of boots ever marched anywhere.

SHOES   The Ultimate Accessory

Heeled, slip-on shoes were designed for evening wear and the mule returned to fashion, this time with a high heel. Barrettes became popular: low-heels were decorated with several bars over the instep, or high-heeled boots were cut open up the front, the edges held by buttoned bars, much like the sandal-boots of the early 2000s.

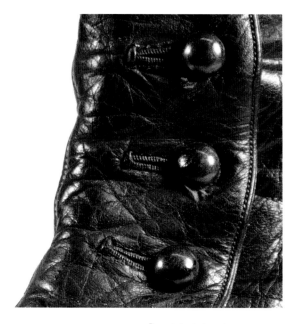

ABOVE: Buttoned boots were, by all accounts, uncomfortable because they did not allow for much flexibility as they clung tightly to the leg. This did not stop fashionable women wearing them. They thought the tight fit was flattering.

RIGHT: In the late nineteenth century, there were concerns that high-heeled boots with narrow toes damaged the feet of women wearing them. The boot shown here has a rounded toe and a sturdy heel. No doubt it fitted an advertisement of the time for boots that "allowed promenading without having to stop and . . . rest the pinched and rebellious feet."

LEFT: The women who wore the buttoned boots of the Late Victorian period required this paraphernalia to help them put their boots on and take them off. A shoehorn was required to fit the foot into the boot; hooks and tweezers essential for doing up and undoing all those fiddly buttons.

Although a method of cutting different soles for right and left feet was introduced in 1801 it came into common usage only in the 1880s. In the United States, Isaac Singer invented a machine in 1856 for sewing leather. More machinery was invented in North America; however, Europeans could not afford to either import the machinery or contravene copyright regulations guarding inventions, so the USA became a leading exporter of factory made shoes. By the start of the First World War (1914–1918), cordwainers had become cobblers, that is to say the repairers, not the makers of shoes.

ABOVE: The ruffled silk is caught in a metal buckle, but the ruffles do not form a latchet neither is the buckle a closure. The arrangement is purely decorative, making an eye-catching evening shoe.

RIGHT: Court shoes became fashionable again as the nineteenth century drew to a close. Very high heels were available but most women fancied low heels. This heel has a straight breast (inner face) and curved outer. The cover is made of silk.

Social changes affected footwear, especially for women who began to demand exercise previously denied them. It started with pedestrianism, but by the 1890s, women were ice-skating, cycling, playing games, and swimming in the sea. Soon, sports footwear was being made for these "New Women."

Products were modeled on men's shoes—the oxford, the brogue, yachting, and running shoes. (Actually, working class women everywhere had always worn clumsy shoes similar to those worn by their men.) Athletic footwear was advanced by Charles Goodyear's 1836 invention of vulcanized rubber. The rubber was "cemented" to the sole without stitching, and this ensured waterproof footwear. Flexible canvas uppers and rubber soles made excellent utility shoes.

LEFT: Shoemakers suffered unemployment as factory-made shoes replaced their handiwork. However, the change did mean that women found employment, working sewing machines for the shoe manufacturers who were building more and more factories as the twentieth century opened.

Bespoke shoes became inordinately expensive and when François Pinet opened a Parisian studio, his lovely footwear was the envy of *tout le monde*. But by the early twentieth century, pretty manufactured high-heeled shoes were being made in the USA—followed by magazine articles warning against the dangers such heels presented to a woman's posture. But most women pooh-poohed such nagging, and rushed to buy mass-produced frivolous shoes.

RIGHT: Rubber soled sports shoes were manufactured initially for boys and young men, but as women began to play games, similar styles were designed for them. A Canadian manufacturer's catalogue of 1901 shows footwear very similar to this tennis player's shoes. It describes them as being made of durable, diced calfskin, with spring heels.

BELOW: Before World War I, manufactured shoes dominated the market, and for the first time, the mass of women could afford pretty footwear. This elegant design of white satin with black velvet and a buckle of rhinestones appears to have whirled many times round the ballroom.

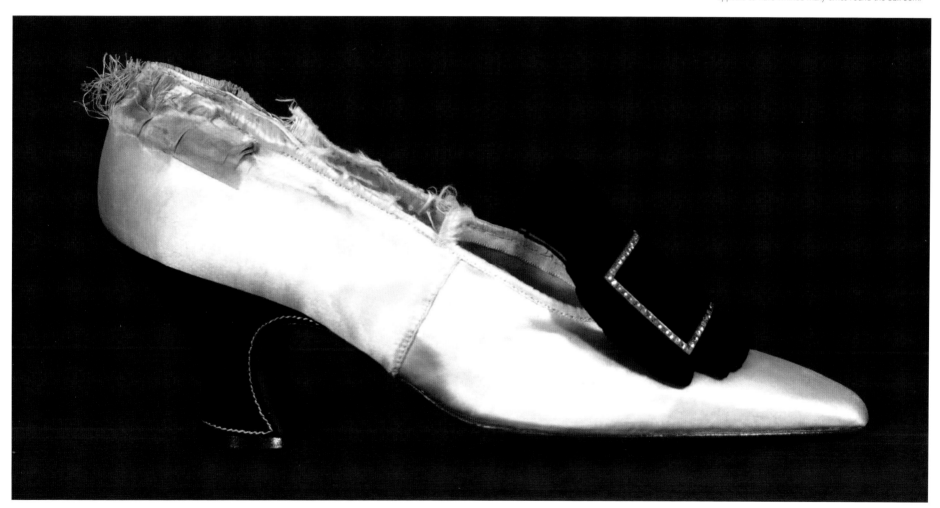

RIGHT: The barrette was a popular and interesting innovation in shoe design. On boots, the cutaway cover strapped the calf, but in this low-heeled version the cutaways pierce the vamp, giving the appearance of sandals but avoiding the perceived immodesty of semi-naked feet. These barrettes are complex in design: stitching and beadwork outline the cut leather and ornament the tongue, while ribbons are used as closure. They are very superior, high quality footwear.

The bespoke shoe continued to be the privilege of the few, and even machine production of quality footwear was beyond the reach of most. However, modern computer technology has made the mass production of footwear available to all economic classes. The twentieth century opened to the promise of wonderful shoes, of high, high heels, of oxfords, brogues, sneakers, and Nikes—all made to delight women everywhere.

RIGHT: The rosette muddles the sharp lines of the fabric, and placed on the vamp, softens the stark effect of the black and white stripes on the cover.

LEFT: This zany, striped court shoe was made by an American manufacturer, and is proof of the quality that could be found in early mass production. It has a Cuban heel and must have been an exciting purchase for working women who, until mechanization, were unable to afford such frivolous, gorgeous footwear. This shoe is a fine forerunner of the splendid choices the twentieth century was to bring to the majority of women.

1920s
DANCING SHOES

The generation who lived through World War I longed to forget the privations they had endured. Have a cocktail, it was said, and have it "quickly while it's still laughing at you." Dancing was all the rage—in London, Paris, and New York people went to *thé dansant* in the afternoon, a dinner dance after the theatre and then on to a nightclub. *Vogue* magazine described the dancing marathon as "a non-stop attaboy" and "a lunatic dash."

RIGHT: All kinds of conventions broke down after The Great War. The rich, fashionable young, bent on pleasure, took to "slumming" in parts of town shunned by their elders. New Yorkers of this class went to Harlem where they could listen to jazz and look at chorus dancers in naughty costumes. At Small's Paradise Club, Harlem, these young women completed their skimpy outfits with big-bowed dancing shoes.

A girl, though, needs the right shoes for dancing —pretty with high heels, but not too high, and designed so they wouldn't fly off capering feet. The 1920s saw the rising popularity of embroidered or patterned shoes held by cross-bars and T-bars. Women were blessed with a choice of delightfully frivolous designs, such as suede overlaid with silver leaves and crimson velvet with gold trim, cut-outs, and intricate straps.

BELOW: These green satin shoes are lined with kid and decorated with rows of silver kid beading. The embroidery was achieved by machine sewing, a huge advance in technology.

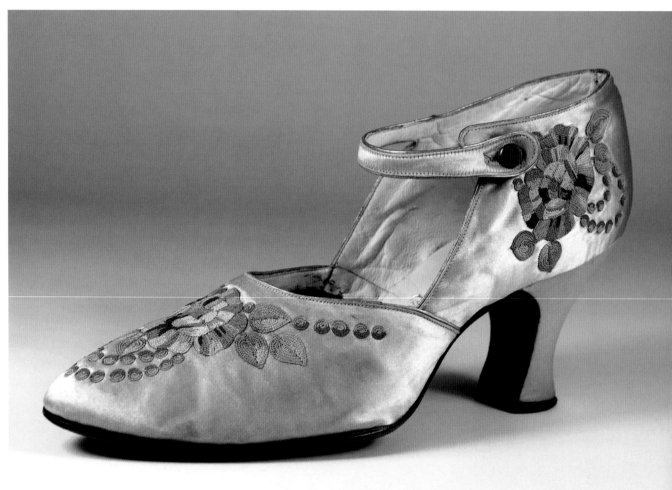

ABOVE: Prior to the twentieth century, embroidery was a slow, skilled handicraft and few women had embroidered footwear. This design typifies the pretty, showy look women wanted from their dancing shoes. The strap is held with a small brass button.

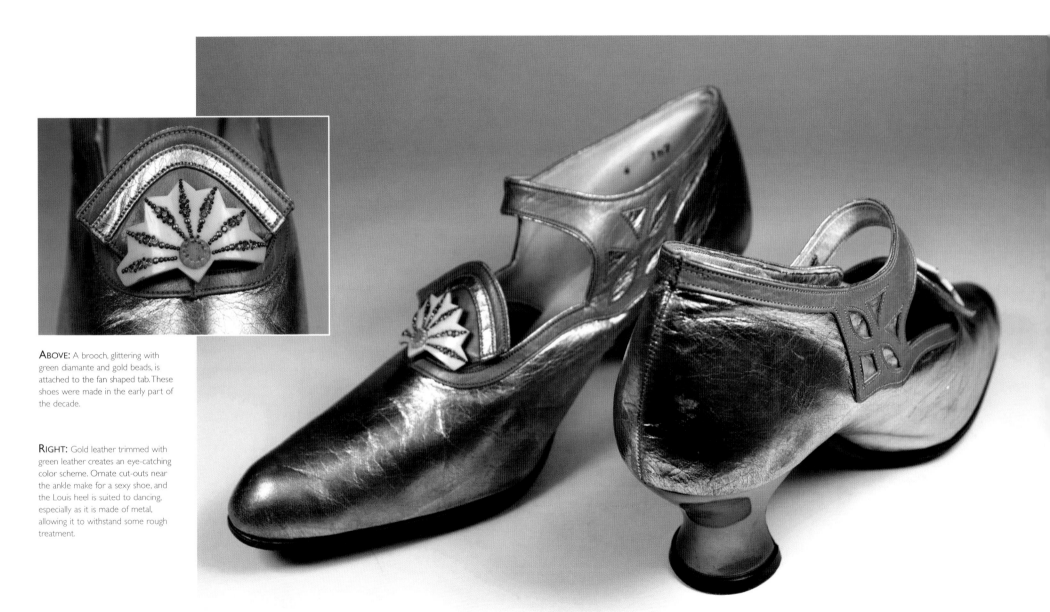

ABOVE: A brooch, glittering with green diamante and gold beads, is attached to the fan shaped tab. These shoes were made in the early part of the decade.

RIGHT: Gold leather trimmed with green leather creates an eye-catching color scheme. Ornate cut-outs near the ankle make for a sexy shoe, and the Louis heel is suited to dancing, especially as it is made of metal, allowing it to withstand some rough treatment.

Music came from the influx of African-American musicians playing tunes and rhythms that amazed young Europeans who had not been exposed to such sounds. And Americans, more familiar with jazz, led the way—as they danced in New York and Chicago, they were imitated by the young dancing in London, Paris, and Berlin. The daring dance performances and costumes of Americans such as Josephine Baker and Florence Mills entranced British and European women. They liberated a generation of girls who had already broken old conventions when they assumed men's work during the war. These black women, however, expressed a new and delightful sense of female independence.

RIGHT: Josephine Baker wears flat-heeled sandals for her dance routine. At the time, footwear that exposed the toes was seen as very bold. The American entertainer entranced all Paris and her infamous banana skirt delighted the crowds. She was unconventional and independent, inspiring young women to be ever more daring in their dress and manners.

Clubs and cabaret cafés rose up in city centers everywhere. Jazz quartets, lively, exotic, and energetic, played from dusk to dawn while the young danced the Charleston to a pulsating drumbeat. Young women wore short dresses that were heavily beaded and fringed. As they pranced around the floor, they were conscious that their shoes were very much on display. Josephine Baker wore shoes made by André Perugia, as did Hollywood film stars, but the needs of non-celebrities were met by mass-produced American imports.

RIGHT: These fuchsia colored shoes were made in England, where contemporary factories were competing against mass production imports from the USA. The pink trim is stitched on and the Louis heels were highly fashionable.

ABOVE: Seymour Troy sold his Troylings with advertisements recommending the brand for its easy-to-wear high heels and ankle straps especially designed not to cut into the flesh. These crocodile skin shoes seem to fulfill both promises, yet they offer elegance and are not sensible-looking comfort footwear.

Seymour
Troy

LEFT: Although this designer was a successful footwear manufacturer, his Troylings proved to be very popular. Inside each shoe, he stamped not only his own company name, but also the Troylings brand name.

BELOW: A double row of stitching secures the fold forming the peep toe on this shoe. The stitches are unobtrusive, but typical of the care that made Troylings a brand that was beautifully designed yet could withstand hard wear.

Seymour Troy was born in Poland but went to the USA when he was very young. He was among thousands of eager Europeans, hopefuls who left the poverty and stifling traditions of their home country to succeed in the New World. In 1923 he opened a small shoe factory. Here he produced a very successful range under the brand name Troylings.

Seymour Troy proved to be a fine designer who was inventive and dedicated to improving the quality and comfort of footwear. He refined measurement in mass-produced shoes when he introduced half-sizes—now standard in footwear manufacture. The shankless shoe and asymmetric strap closures were the inventions of Seymour Troy, and his high-cut Valkyrie was so popular it was copied by many of his competitors. In 1960 he became the first winner of the Mercury Award, given by the National Shoe Industry Association. He retired in 1975.

The newfangled gramophone meant that music could be brought into the home. The romantic novelist Barbara Cartland recalled being a house-guest in a country house and seeing records put on the gramophone the moment she and her fellow guests arrived. Everyone danced before dinner, after dinner, and even in the afternoon. Gorgeous shoes that were beaded or embroidered and had interesting straps were important items in the weekend bag of any well-dressed young debutante.

Machine embroidery had been perfected. Shoppers could find brown suede bedecked with golden stitched leaves and little gold buckles on the T-strap, or black velvet that was covered in pink embroidery and had black bows on the crossbar. The Americans manufactured beaded shoes, while leather dyes had improved allowing daring color mixes or painted designs.

RIGHT: Andre Perugia was a famous designer and skilled cordwainer. His Parisian workshop was besieged by women who would not dream of buying mass-produced footwear. He designed this elegant shoe: it is perfectly balanced in construction and quietly adorned with a gold stitched tab.

BELOW: The shimmering brocade cover of this shoe is patterned in a contemporary abstract of grays, greens, and pinks. The heel is set with pastes and enamels in a geometry of colored dots and lines. The shoe is stamped "Leicester," implying a factory product.

BELOW: A shoe for afternoon wear is made in pale leather with a snakeskin inset. Thin laces tie the ghillie fastening and the heel is leather covered. This footwear came from the factory of James Beattie Ltd in Wolverhampton, England.

The Englishman Moses Manfield had built an imposing factory in Northampton, and worked hard to compete with the imports from across the Atlantic. Initially his products were dull and sensible, but by the 1920s he was selling his elegant, well-made shoes in outlets across Britain and Europe.

Of course, the rich continued to yearn for bespoke or handmade footwear and they found it in Paris. Wealthy American heiresses flocked to the city in search of special shoes. The shoemaker François Pinet embroidered his silk uppers and emphasized his cross-bars with stitching in contrasting colors. Other cordwainers hand painted silk uppers and preferred shoes with extravagant decoration. Many of these had high vamps onto which were laid rows, circles, and squiggles of steel-cut beads and rhinestones.

LEFT: For this particular shoe, the customer was supplied with a protective cover to tie over the buckle when the shoe was stored.

Beautifully embroidered dancing shoes were imported from China. They fulfilled the fashion demands of the day, having long narrow vamps held by cross bars. The shoes were not labeled by the designer or the manufacturer, and were made for export and the small number of Chinese women who preferred to wear western clothes.

The Italian Pietro Yantorny opened a salon in Paris and hung up a sign advertising "The World's Most Expensive Shoes." His footwear was exquisitely crafted, and he favored fabrics such as velvet, antique lace, brocade, or reptile skin. The atmosphere of elitism was increased by the fact that clients were expected to wait two years while Yantorny constructed their shoes. A superb craftsman, he was illiterate and sometimes his name was spelt as Yantomi or Yantoumi, but Yantorny was used on his business card.

LEFT: A bespoke shoe has always been an expensive purchase, and the value of this 1920s shoe was increased by the use of precious stones on the buckle.

Another Italian working in Paris was André Perugia, who made shoes for the French *haute couture* houses of Elsa Schiaparelli and Poiret. The Polish cordwainer Seymour Troy found success in the USA. He was an inventive designer and introduced half-sizes into shoe measurements. All these men made beautiful shoes in silks and velvets for the richest party girls of the 1920s.

LEFT: Faux stones adorn the gilt buckle of the shoe and an orange fan of crepe surrounds it. Historians believe this fan decoration was added as a theatrical trimming and was not part of the original shoe design.

ABOVE: Fashionable evening shoes were extravagant and frivolous, suited to the post-war mood of determined gaiety. Yellow silk gives this shoe brilliance and makes it a dancing shoe to covet. A mother-of-pearl button fastens the instep bar.

Pietro
Yantorny

As a boy Yantorny was apprenticed to numerous cordwainers in Naples, before going on to study in Nice, Paris, and London. He was inclined to embellish his life with colorful stories and claimed grand official positions, but archives after his death reveal a picture of hardship. However, he was a proud man: when he opened his workshop in Paris in 1904 he refused all but the wealthiest clients.

Yantorny sought inspiration for his designs in the museums of the French capital. Although reputed to be illiterate, his eye was keen, and he was able to incorporate historical references in the elaborate ornament he favored for his shoes. His work particularly reflects the aesthetics of the eighteenth century. During the Depression Yantorny closed his business and went traveling round India. He returned to France in 1932, and died there four years later.

LEFT: The sharply pointed toes found in eighteenth century shoes are not repeated here, but Yantorny has copied the kid heel so popular in that century and the latchet closure with a buckle. But he has modified his modern version with a small buckle and a long tongue.

ABOVE: The swirling tongue and the rich embroidery of curved shapes express this designer's deep knowledge and love of the French Baroque style of the eighteenth century.

RIGHT: Yantorny shows his signature touches in this elegant shoe. It has the narrow vamp he prefers, and the latchet and buckle closure he admired when he visited museums to study the footwear of the eighteenth century.

LEFT: The close-up of the high heel reveals the subtle mottled effect of reptile skin.

BELOW: On this handcrafted white kid footwear, dark snakeskin is patterned to create an elegant afternoon shoe. The insets of triangular points are smart and snappy, and the instep bar ensures a comfortable fit. It is stamped N.Greco, who was a much admired European shoemaker during this decade.

Dressy afternoon shoes were usually made of leather, but even so they tended to be heavily decorated. Black and bronze leather was entwined to emphasize edges or crossbars. On crossbars, eyelets replaced loops and twisted cord was used to tie the bars. Afternoon shoes were high heeled and, as with evening shoes, straps and cut-outs were favored. They came in black patent leather or suede, and were sometimes trimmed with white kid or grosgrain ribbon.

Narrow shoes with an exaggerated tongue, trimmed with a buckle, or demure snakeskin with a cross bar appealed as everyday wear to many shoppers. Ferragamo designed a high-cut pump in alternating bands of suede and leather and a straight high heel. While these individual cordwainers and designers worked from their workshops, British and German manufacturers were desperate to catch up with American mass production.

ABOVE: More and more young women were allowed employment in offices, and this business-like footwear must have given them confidence as they marched into a male world, previously denied to females. It is a Gibson shoe with a rounded bulldog, or Boston toe. The five-eyelet fastening has wide silk laces, and the shoe has a Cuban heel. The shiny patent leather adds to its important air and appearance.

The Rayne company had a factory in North London and opened a shoe store in the high-end shopping boulevard, Bond Street. In Germany the Salamander Company manufactured shoes out of a factory near Stuttgart, and it remains the largest shoe manufacturer in Germany. Both companies determined to produce well-designed and beautiful shoes as fine as any from the USA.

ABOVE: Satin was favored for the cover of evening shoes. This design seems plain and simple, relying on the sheen of the textile to give a rich effect. A paste button holds the instep bar, but the lacquered heels glitter with diamante decoration.

In the wider world there were new arenas that women sought to conquer, such as sport and gymnastics. In fact, after World War I there was a positive craze for fitness. Also, the skimpy straight dresses and the jersey knits promoted by Chanel demanded a slender body that was "flexible and tubular."

Women played tennis, stood on their heads, swung from trapezes and went golfing. *Vogue* carried photographs of duchesses swinging their athletic legs in the air or balancing on the muscular shoulders of an instructor. The French writer Colette even had her own mini-gymnasium in her Paris apartment. Here she vaulted over leather gym horses and somersaulted across the floor!

LEFT: These Louis heels are made of wood, then decorated with colored, pearlized plastic. The pattern makes vague reference to Ancient Egyptian design, although the colors are thoroughly modern in their brightness and clarity.

François
Pinet

François Pinet learnt the craft of cordwainer from his father. In 1855 he opened his first shop in Paris at 44, rue Paradis Poissonière. His skills were quickly recognized, especially as he was clever enough to design shoes to complement contemporary dress fashions. He favored the Louis heel, but made his higher than the conventional model. Beautiful embroidery decorated both his shoes and his boots, and his T-bar evening shoes were famous for their prettiness. He employed over a hundred people in his workshops, and twice that number of outworkers (who embroidered and stitched). Pinet's own son later took over the business and under his management the company expanded. During the 1920s the Pinet brand opened in London, Berlin, Vienna, and New York. Although the company was busy throughout the Depression years of the 1930s, it did not survive World War II.

LEFT: Pinet was a superb designer, one of the very first to be recognized for his contribution to footwear. This 1867 boot has a textile leg—surely more flexible and comfortable for the wearer than the usual tight leather. But the vamp and heel are given leather covers because that material is more waterproof than a textile. The boot is marked with his name.

ABOVE: This high-heeled oxford has, in the brogue style, a charming decoration of stamped seams. The five pairs of eyes are threaded with thick laces that make a showy tie. Pinet brought lashings of chic to a standard conventional design. The shoe was made c.1912.

RIGHT: This shoe justifies Pinet's reputation for creating, year after year, fresh and exciting designs. It was made in 1955 and carries a bold decoration on the vamp but, obviously, the shoe is eye-catching because it has no heel. The foot is supported by a metal strut inside the shoe. This extraordinary design was a bespoke shoe— few manufacturers would risk investment in such unconventional footwear.

The French tennis player Suzanne Lenglen, who was known as "La Divine," dominated the women's game. She won twenty-five grand slams, but she was loved as much for her dress sense as for her sportsmanship. Lenglen was graceful, elegant, and stylish. The crowd gasped at her sleeveless, thigh-high tennis dresses designed by the couturier Jean Patou.

As a beautiful athlete, Lenglen inspired fashionable women and female athletes but also encouraged the development of sportswear and footwear. Movie shots show her twirling on the tennis court and wearing what appear to be white canvas shoes. These tennis shoes were known as sneakers in the USA and plimsolls in Britain, and sold in enormous numbers across the globe.

LEFT: The camera captures Suzanne Lenglen as she springs across the tennis court. She was a French tennis champion, but her shoes here were probably of American manufacture. The USA was in the forefront of sportswear, and produced a white buckskin shoe with rubber soles that was highly recommended as footwear for tennis players.

Manufacturers were quick to provide shoes for all sporty activities. *Vogue* reassured its readers, telling them it was fine to wear such "clumsy" shoes. An American advertisement issued in the early 1920s illustrated the Bulldog, a canvas ankle boot trimmed with leather on a rubber sole, and the Bathing, a narrow, simple canvas lace-up shoe which looked remarkably like a modern sneaker or plimsoll. Europeans were quick to make copies.

The United States Rubber Company presented their Snug-Ler, a moccasin-style felt cover with rubber soles. Another manufacturer made a tan elk skin walking shoe with a laced vamp closure and, of course, a rubber sole. White buckskin lace-ups with a red rubber sole were sold as tennis shoes. The forerunner of athletic shoes for both men and women can be found in the All Star, a tan canvas, rubber-soled ankle shoe with a long tongue and a row of eyelets threaded with a sturdy shoelace. This model was made by the American company Converse in 1919.

BELOW: Early sports shoes for women often copied the style of menswear as revealed in the brogued seams of this footwear. But these 1920 front-lacing shoes are made of soft, pliable leather and have rubber soles. Women tennis players in particular favored them on the court.

RIGHT: As factory production made shoes in more abundance and variety than craft methods, women were able to build a shoe wardrobe. Indoor footwear for intimate domestic wear became a possibility. The slippers of the 1920s were not for careless dressers: they came with flattering little heels and were made from fragile textiles, such as satin. This would then be quilted and, often, trimmed with fur, but the throat of this red slipper has a braid trim that twists into a flower on the vamp.

There was a further interesting development in footwear when the slipper came into being. The word slipper had formerly been used to describe those dressy evening shoes that "slipped on," but now the term came to define indoor, boudoir wear. These slippers were not homely and comfortable things in which to shuffle about the kitchen: they had little heels, came in quilted pink satin or silk, and fluffy fur trimmed the throat.

And of course the mule returned, now with high heels. The rich young woman swayed from her bed to the bathroom and then the dressing room or, on intimate mornings, she sashayed off to breakfast wearing her high-heeled slippers.

The 1920s was a decade of frivolity and extravagant pleasures, and footwear reflected the times. Never before had women been able to pick and choose from such a large variety of beautifully made shoes.

LEFT: American manufacturers came up with shoeboxes as an efficient way of packing and selling footwear. This 1920s shoe store is lined with boxes, each labeled to identify style and size, so that, with speed and ease, the assistant could find and pull out the desired pair of shoes. Customers rested in comfortable chairs while they were being served. Meanwhile, the sombre interior gave the shop gravitas.

1930s
GLAMOUR AND DEMOCRACY

After the extravagance and excess of the 1920s, the 1930s had a grim beginning. The Wall Street Crash of 1929 was followed by the Depression, with mass unemployment in most western economies. Nevertheless people still had to go about their daily routines, while the rich who'd been spared the fallout of the Crash hardly seemed aware of the hardship around them.

The passion for gymnastics moved beyond an elite circle of wealthy women. Now many women were enthusiastic about sport and physical activities. They gathered in large groups to practice "synchronized exercise," during which they stood in rows and coordinated their movements, and as they did so, they were grateful for flexible canvas shoes. They admired the tomboy spirit displayed by Katherine Hepburn in the movie *Little Women*, and tramped about in waterproof galoshes, which had first been produced in the nineteenth century. They were thrilled when Gloria Swanson was seen driving a car—the first female movie star to be seen performing this daring act. This delighted many, but a small band of women were truly inspired and actually took to motor racing.

RIGHT: Previously confined to a leisured elite, physical exercise became a widespread activity among women working in factories and offices, and they joined organized groups for instruction. Their schoolgirl dresses seem comical when viewed from the twenty-first century, and their shoes woefully inadequate. Some wear sandals, some plimsolls or sneakers, while others are in walking shoes. Well-designed, ergonomic footwear was not available for these hopeful athletes.

Women had acted as ambulance drivers throughout World War I, and in the United States there had been a "ladies only" race as early as 1917. It was an expensive, dangerous sport, but by 1930 the technology had greatly improved and women refused to be put off by male arguments against their participation.

BELOW: Lace-tied shoes remained popular as daytime wear, but not all were plain and sensible in appearance. This comfortable black shoe, with its sturdy heel, is given perky touches of red laces and trims. This footwear suited country tweeds and active, everyday life.

Kay Petre won the championship on the Brooklands Ladies' Outer Circuit in England in 1934, while the novelist Barbara Cartland was a keen participant in the sport. But the most exciting "speederette"—as the lady racers were called—

was Hellé Nice. A gorgeous adventuress from France, Hellé was an athlete, trapeze artist, and major racing champion in Europe, America, and South Africa between 1929 and 1949. The Italian carmaker Bugatti supported her motoring career.

BELOW: Hellé Nice, the glamorous "speederette," leans against her Bugatti racing car. At the time, her trousers were considered very bold. Her shoes, shaped like masculine slip-on slippers, were unusual and probably made from soft kid leather. Her ensemble is unquestionably suitable for motor racing.

Photographs show the speederettes in simple flat slippers with a thick cross bar placed close to the ankle, or in low-heeled oxfords. The latter were usually made of leather but a few ladies sported canvas sports brogues with low but sturdy heels. Hellé Nice was snapped in a dashing pair of two-tone brogues called co-respondents, but known in the USA as saddle shoes. The tongue and latchets were in tan leather against a cream upper. Fashion illustrations presented driving clothes with images of young women in then-daring trousers and high heels with T-bars, but in the world outside fashion magazines, variations of the saddle shoe were sold by the thousand during the 1930s.

There were high-heeled copies of saddle shoes but they were no good for stomping across the golf course or even for a spectator at the motor racing. Two-tones, in any form, were perceived as simply elegant, and when they came with a high heel they made a perfect town or afternoon shoe.

LEFT: These shoes are a variation on the usual design of the spectator where normally the toe box and heel were in dark tones. But they reveal the comfort and visual appeal of two-tone shoes.

LEFT: Manufacturers were dumbfounded by the generation of emancipated sportswomen and, lacking any experience, could only modify men's styles for physically active women. These well-worn and dignified day shoes are simply men's brogues given a narrow vamp and a medium high heel.

ABOVE: This extraordinary shoe defies analysis and is typical of Perugia's originality of design. Here is an upturned Ottoman toe, but the embroidered vamp has European leaf motifs and an Inca-type green skull. The cut-away arch demands some daring from his contemporary market—but then he designed it in 1927 when young women longed to be bold.

André
Perugia

André Perugia, an Italian who grew up in Nice, was taught shoemaking by his father. His early work was displayed in a hotel foyer where it was spotted by the Parisian couturier, Paul Poiret. After he finished his war service as an airplane engineer, Perugia looked up Poiret. It was the start of a design partnership and Perugia made shoes for Josephine Baker and the dancers at the Folies Bergère. Rita Hayworth and Gloria Swanson were among his clients. He expanded to Nice, and went into collaboration with Elsa Schiaparelli.

Perugia's artistic inspiration came from the Orient, modern art, and industrial design and his shoes were always beautiful in color, design, and structure. The Rayne company in Great Britain and I. Miller in the USA commissioned him. His articulate wooden heel and interchangeable heels were admired innovations. During the 1960s he was technical advisor to Charles Jourdan, who later inherited Perugia's archives.

ABOVE: Perugia was never predictable. This shoe is from 1920; it is not daring or radical but has unusual details. A faux tongue of modern geometric design transforms this modest, narrow vamped black court shoe.

RIGHT: It is not hard to understand why women longed for shoes from Perugia. His designs were both conventional and unexpected. On this pair, the vamp has been extended and given a subtle upward curve.

SHOES   The Ultimate Accessory

Another great heroine of this decade was the American aviatrix, Amelia Earhart, whose courage in this very masculine occupation inspired and amazed everyone. She was slim, boyish but very stylish, and designed a line of women's clothing for "easy living." Her garments were actually modified men's clothes and included plaid shirts, jodhpurs, and pleated pants. She was frequently photographed in her pilot's overalls and, to the delight of female readers of newspapers and magazines she looked extremely feminine in this male outfit. She also appears to have favored masculine-style, front-lacing ankle boots.

RIGHT: Amelia Earheart wears clothes more commonly seen on airmen. Women did not wear leather coats and earflap caps, and even her long laced boots were not of the sexy variety but utility male footwear. However, her beauty and elegance dispelled any hint of rough masculinity in her appearance, and this encouraged other women to seek practicality over fashion.

The English aviatrix, Amy Johnson, had similar style and swank. Reports from the time tell us that "she dressed for record-breaking as if for a lunch date." Was Amy Johnson piloting her flimsy little 1930s airplane while wearing gorgeous strappy high heels?

For sandals had, as the 1920s ended, become acceptable in respectable society. This was thanks to the shoe designer Salvatore Ferragamo, who had invented the metal arch support. This meant that the shoe toe-cap was no longer needed as a brake to prevent the foot from slipping. Now straps were wrapped like jewelry round the bare foot, and the foot became as decorative as the shoe itself.

LEFT: Women were as energetic on the dance floor as the exercise field, although pretty shoes were preferred for the first activity. A shoe held by a T-strap and supported by a thick high heel made for sure footed dancing, but this shoe would tempt a market beyond that of dancers only. The combination of black and silver, with unusual cut-outs on the vamp, is stunning.

ABOVE: This shoe has intricate details of a fringed vamp, exaggerated looped eyelets, and silver lining. The heel is over five inches, higher than was generally preferred, so probably the shoe was designed for attending cocktail or dinner parties, and not for use on the dance floor.

Dancing continued to be a major preoccupation in this decade, but now big swing bands provided the music. London crowds filled the Hammersmith Palais de Dance and the Astoria in Charing Cross. Here they jitterbugged, tangoed, and danced the rhumba.

The American movie stars and ballroom dancers, Fred Astaire and Ginger Rogers, persuaded moviegoers that they too could look suave and graceful on the dance floor. So confident was Astaire of the popularity of ballroom dancing that he traveled across the Atlantic to give demonstrations and classes in London. Everywhere female dance students searched for copies of the peep-toes and high-heeled sandals that Ginger Rogers wore.

LEFT: The famous movie dancing couple, Ginger Rogers and Fred Astaire, strut their stuff in the movie, *Swing Time*. Unusually, she wears court shoes without an ankle strap or T-bar, but the heels are sturdy. Astaire wears spats, white coverings meant to protect men's shoes outdoors but, instead, became fashionable indoor wear in the '30s.

Dance shoes were less frivolous than those of the '20s Charleston girls, indeed many shoes lost their visual impact altogether. The thick high heel continued to be popular, but decoration was now sober. The straps of sandals compensated for this but most shoes relied on contrast stitching, or laces in a complementary color to decorate the uppers. Brocade uppers were used, though in quiet tones. Evening shoes relied on an open cut, ankle straps, and color to give them flair. Clothes were more careful and sober in their cut than the narrow, beaded tubes of the '20s: skirts were below the knee, the fabric pleated or folded.

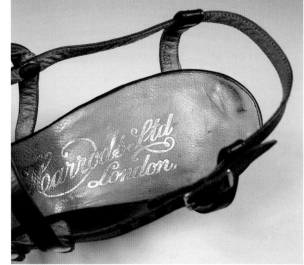

ABOVE: Sandals imported from Czechoslovakia and Mexico threatened home markets. The footwear was crafted from embellished leather and intricately braided straps. American and English manufacturers were quick to copy the look. However, this imitation did not rely on craftsmen to weave and mark the leather, but used color as decoration and imitated the complexity of the imported sandals with the use of numerous straps, attached with metallic studs.

RIGHT: The instep is marked with the name, Harrods, a world famous English department store. Following the custom of the time, the manufacturer does not acknowledge the designer.

Textiles were used to add a note of color to the overall mood of restraint. Velvet and satin shoes created a quietly sumptuous look, as did gold lamé peeping below long, sensuous gowns. These rich fabrics suited the draped, sophisticated dresses worn by movie stars such as Bette Davis and Jean Harlow. On the one hand actresses created an image of poise, beauty, and self-reliance, but on the other they played circus performers, sharp newspaper girls, or crooked *femmes fatales*. They were feisty rather than respectable, and their shoes were as smart as they were.

LEFT: This beautiful dance shoe has, fortunately, been well preserved. Stamped Hellstem and mass-produced, the patterned turquoise brocade is trimmed with gold braid and the buckle is covered with diamante. The arch is sexily exposed and the heel is the perfect height for dancing.

Adidas

Adolf and Rudi Dessler were enterprising German brothers. In 1910, they recycled motor tires and rucksacks into rubber-soled canvas shoes, and in 1924, opened The Dassler Brothers Shoe Factory in Herzogenraurach, Germany where they specialized in sports footwear. Their reputation was sealed when Jesse Owens, the American athlete, wore Dassler shoes for the Berlin Olympics in 1936.

After World War II, the brothers parted: Rudi called his company Puma and Adi renamed the once-shared Dassler company Adidas. The latter's sales escalated when they were promoted by competitors in the 1956 Melbourne Olympics, and also when Adidas became the official footwear suppliers to the Munich Olympics in 1972. Adidas remained the world's major sports footwear manufacturer until the 1980s, when Nike and Reebok entered the field. Like other manufacturers, Adidas relocated to Asia in the '90s but struggled to hold a place in a competitive market filled with sports shoe products.

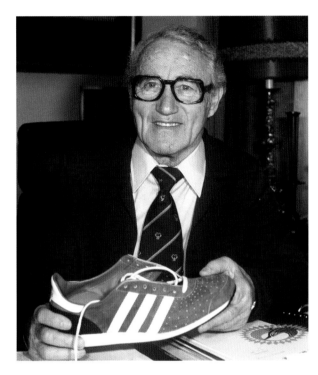

ABOVE: Adi Dassler, the founder of Adidas footwear, shows off one of his products. He and his son, Horst, built Adidas into the most successful company in sports footwear. Adi died in 1978, just as Adidas was faced with new, but fierce competition in its field of specialized footwear manufacture.

RIGHT: These trainers appeared in the 1980s. The sole is thick and, of interest to women's footwear, it slopes in from the toe, making the footwear capable of quick, easy movement. This kind of detail, important to athletes, was to be used to improve the high-heeled platform of the twenty-first century.

LEFT: Jesse Owens, a black American, famously beat the pale representatives of the Aryan Master Race—as his European competitors were called by the German Nazis at the 1936 Berlin Olympics. It was ironic that Owens won medals for sprinting and long jump while wearing athletic footwear made by the Dassler Brothers, the German company that evolved into Adidas.

BELOW: Ferragamo released a burst of daring creativity among his fellow designers. When he presented his platform shoes for the entertainer, Carmen Miranda, others followed with experimental soles. Naked toes were no longer considered immodest. This gorgeous webbing of gold straps attached to a blatantly ridged platform was one of the more alluring designs to emerge in this period. It comes from the workshop of N. Greco of Paris.

The English manufacturer Bally sold a high-heeled sandal with silver and black suede straps. Other houses produced peep-toes, cut-away vamps, and ankle straps in suede of various colors. Day shoes were narrow with high vamps of woven leather enhanced with touches of painted decoration, or trimmed with contrast stitch. Usually they were dark in color and carried little ornament. They looked smart, while conveying an air of confidence and efficiency.

Ferragamo produced crocheted gold cellophane sling backs, while Perugia created a dashing high-heeled sandal. He made the platform and heel pale blue, while the straps of the upper were plum-colored. And thanks to the relaxed style and manners of the Americans, day sandals made a major comeback during the 1930s. Ferragamo created some beautiful examples and his designs certainly stimulated the trend.

ABOVE: This pair of quality shoes was produced for the high end of the market frequented by women who, though conservative in style, were also fashionable. The interesting strap fitting and the heels pay heed to current vogues, but the materials and craftsmanship, and the engraved buckle, lift the shoe from the general mass of products.

BELOW: This sandal is made of wood and fabric. The wooden sole under the toes comprises three sections, allowing for flexibility not possible with a solid piece of wood. The heels are oddly wider than the sole, probably for a quirky design note rather than for any functional purpose.

André Perugia startled the world with his "Cubist" sandal, in which the shank was divided into two sections, placing the heel right under the arch. His Turban sandal of pleated and knotted leather and his Mask of snakeskin, made in 1929, were revolutionary.

But Ferragamo led the market with raffia-bound sandals decorated with raffia flowers and gave these concoctions heels constructed from wine corks. This designer popularized wedgies and platform heels. He started with cork but was soon creating platform soles with mosaics of glass or stripes of colored suede. Others such as Vivier, Perugia and Hollywood costume designers were soon making equally flamboyant sandals.

British and European women in lower income groups relied on shoe manufacturers such as Raynes, Salamander, and the hugely successful Czech company, Bata, for their footwear. American women had more numerous choices, but of course, all were led by trends from Hollywood and French designers; their options were wide ranging and embraced sandals, sling-backs, sneakers, loafers, and hiking boots.

RIGHT: Ferragamo became famous with his invention of the wedge heel. He introduced it in the '30s but the style was to become very popular in the '40s. At first the shape was a simple triangular sole, but he went on to layer the thick sole giving it an interesting silhouette, as in the black suede wedgie shown here.

Salvatore
Ferragamo

This Italian designer was an apprentice cordwainer in Italy but went to the USA when he was sixteen years old. There he studied anatomy and methods of leather dyeing. He opened a workshop in California where he designed footwear for the movies. He also invented his steel arch support that greatly reduced the discomfort of high-heeled shoes. He returned to Italy in 1925 but during his country's war with Abyssinia (now Ethiopia) leather shortages inspired Ferragamo to use wood, cork, cellophane, and raffia.

Ferragamo revolutionised shoe design in a number of ways and his flair and originality attracted royalty and movie stars who flocked to his headquarters in Florence. His was a family business and on his death his daughter presented her designs for the company. She and her four siblings became directors and the Ferragamo brand continues to be a major Italian maker and exporter of high-end footwear.

ABOVE: By 1990, the date on the shoe detailed above, Ferragamo's name conjured up qualities of fine Italian craftsmanship and superb design. Many women dreamt of having a pair of shoes bearing the curvy line of the Ferragamo stamp.

LEFT: Here is a shoe to melt the heart of even the most unromantic person. Ferragamo made it in the 1950s, knowing the stiletto heel gave his creation high sex appeal while the pale cover of delicate beadwork would make it utterly beautiful.

RIGHT: The master tests the structure of a strappy high-heeled mule, slipping it over a protective bootie on a model's foot. His expression reveals his pleasure at the creation of yet another beautiful shoe.

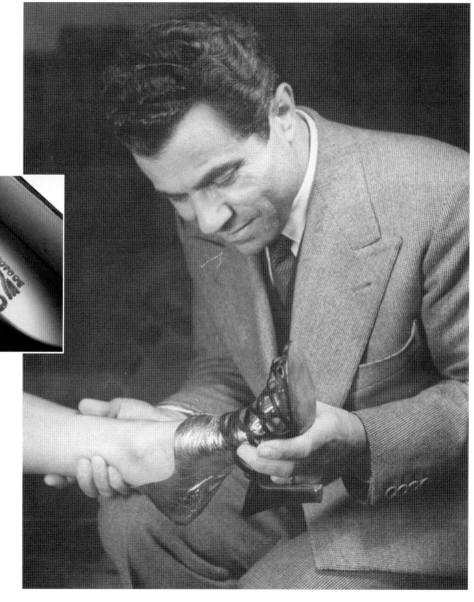

While the fashionistas of California, Miami, and the French Riviera frolicked on the beaches or played gentle games of tennis, sportswomen presented themselves for the 1936 Berlin Olympics. Clothes and shoe manufacturers responded to the needs of the athletes and those who admired them. The Englishman Joseph Foster had been making spiked running shoes for some time, while Paul Sperry in America produced his boating shoe, the slip resistant Top-Sider. The German company, the Dassler Brothers Shoe Factory (later to become Adidas), had begun manufacturing before World War I, making sports shoes from discarded canvas rucksacks and rubber tires.

BELOW: Perhaps the Californian sunshine inspired a love of color, or perhaps it was the glamour of Hollywood, but in the '30s, Ferragamo, Perugio, and their followers delighted in the use of hot, vibrant color. These wedgies were surely made in homage to Ferragamo's original striped wedgies, and the gold toe and ankle straps certainly add a glitzy movie star touch.

BELOW: Manufacturers were keen to develop sports shoes but, at this stage, didn't pay much attention to the physical needs of sportswomen. This design is derived directly from the shoes made for male golfers but the fussy fringed tongue-cum-tassle is pleasing, and a girl could use them for everyday wear as well as out on the golf course.

In the 1920s the brothers set up business as the manufacturers of shoes for different sports. The Berlin Olympics gave the company wonderful publicity, especially as the American champion Jesse Owens raced in "Dasslers" and won four gold medals. Of course, keen sportsmen and women were delighted by this development in footwear, especially as other manufacturers started to produce similar goods.

Other developments in Germany were not so pleasant. The Nazis were in power and in 1938 took the country and all of Europe into war. When France fell in 1940, *Vogue* magazine, previously very snooty about the influence of Hollywood and the movie stars, had to look to the USA for fashion trends and direction.

RIGHT: This wood and textile shoe has a naif handmade appearance. The textile straps are nailed to the sole, and they are arranged in a simple cross from arch to toe, plus a couple of loops to hold a tying lace. But the use of non-leather materials would make such constructions an important design source in the next decade.

Looking at back numbers of *Vogue*, it seems that it willfully ignored the democratic glamour of the movies. Apparently its editors could not comprehend a world where class and aristocratic titles did not matter. They seemed impervious to the views of thousands of women who wanted a world where good looks and intelligence could bring wealth and prestige, regardless of the circumstances of birth.

LEFT: Glamour and experimentation were characteristic of the decade and this footwear typifies these traits. The black suede evening shoe is perforated, threaded, and given a furled throat. But the shank is unusually long, threatening an uncomfortable fit. This is an interesting experiment in shape that never proved popular, although the shoe is of elegant appearance. It is stamped Lotus American Last.

RIGHT: Pretty shoes were not readily available during the war years, and rationing was strict. No wonder these young women seem eager to swap their precious clothes coupons for sexy ankle straps while discarded closed court shoes, lie on the floor.

1940s
AUSTERITY AND INVENTION

At the start of World War II, *Vogue* noted: "Last year women were running households. This year they are running canteens, voluntary organizations, service units—and taking orders as well as giving them."

Not only were women donning uniform, they were faced with clothing rations. German women had to apply in person for permission to buy shoes. In the USA rationing applied only to leather shoes, but in Britain clothing ration coupons had to cover all a woman's yearly purchases, including shoes.

Of course rationing combined with shortages of leather and rubber forced shoemakers everywhere to look for alternative materials. They responded with footwear made of textiles, plastic, or raffia. Suede and reptile skins were relatively abundant because none was suitable for army boots (and therefore restricted), so manufacturers began to use these materials in both shoes and handbags.

Stockings, too, were scarce in Europe, and women were reluctant to expose their bare feet in sling-backs or peep-toed shoes. (In Britain, anyway, peep toes were forbidden under the rationing system.) Young women treasured their nylons for special occasions, when their men took a break from the war in Europe and came home to dine and dance. But for everyday wear, the oxford was favored, though with a medium or Cuban heel. The high vamp and comfortable heel height suited women who were on their feet for much of the day, walking, or cycling to work, and shopping, as well as at home.

The oxfords of the early 1940s do have a very sensible look: nurses and teachers liked their comfort and modest appearance. The shoe had a walled toe and high narrow vamp. Some were decorated with a fringed or saddle-stitched tongue, while others had same-fabric bows laid on the vamp. The style persisted into the 1950s, bought by those who wanted their shoes to be practical and not gorgeously silly. By the mid-1940s a round toe on the oxford became fashionable, a precursor to the baby-doll pump sold at the end of the decade. Nevertheless, the so-called spectator, which used white suede and a little dark leather trimming, maintained its popularity.

ABOVE: A high standard of workmanship was maintained among some British manufacturers, despite the limitations imposed by war conditions. A flattering high heel and a carefully formed vamp decoration make for a quality design.

RIGHT: A shortage of leather in the '40s drove manufacturers to improvise with materials. Reptile skins were easier to find than leather, but this shoe has made a very pleasing combination of both materials. The straight heel was very popular.

ABOVE: Elegant evening shoes were available for those who wanted to use their ration coupons to purchase them. This shoe is made with suede and printed textile, both inexpensive and available to government-assigned British "Utility" shoe manufacturers. The latchet closure tied with a broad ribbon makes a pleasing reference to historic styles.

Vogue gave advice on "austerity chic" and showed their readers how to polish their shoes. Besides, at the news that a boyfriend or husband would be home on leave, even the busiest WAAF and WASP found time for chic, time to apply lipstick, and don a pair of sexy, strappy shoes.

Manufacturers did offer alternatives to the dull wartime look, made to follow government rules.

Sandals need less material than closed footwear, and an unnamed British manufacturer made a zany high-heeled sandal of synthetic strips in yellow and red. Plastic discs were fitted between the inner and outer soles, and the effect was charming. Ferragamo used packing string to weave an enchanting sandal, while Perugia produced sandals of startling color. More successful than the sandal, though, was the wedgie.

LEFT: These cork-soled sandals are held to the foot with a single broad band over the arch. Evins has made a daring color combination, edging the wide maroon band with a pale orange border, and this makes a pleasing punctuation mark to the greens of the beach outfit.

BELOW: Evins has designed shoes to complement the shimmering garment and stockings of the outfit. The open-vamped shoes are silver-white with a square sequinned buckle, and the heels, curved into the shank, are translucent acrylic. They are glamorous footwear, without any of the usual accompanying problems of toe-pinching or uncomfortable height.

David
Evins

By birth an Englishman, David Evins moved to the USA when he was a child. He started as an illustrator in New York, before studying pattern making while working as an independent designer. Evins served in the U.S. Army Signal Corps and, at the end of the war, opened a design studio with his brother. Their work was soon commissioned by I. Miller, the shoe manufacturer.

Evins was recognized as a master craftsman, and his clients included Ava Gardner and Marlene Dietrich as well as every president's wife from Mamie Eisenhower to Nancy Reagan. Evins had a knack of designing footwear to suit the wearer's personality. He was an innovator, being the first to use Velcro to secure ankle straps: he even used the metal stems of trophies as heels. He was commissioned by major houses such as Valentino, Ralph Lauren, and Calvin Klein, but also designed for the mass market.

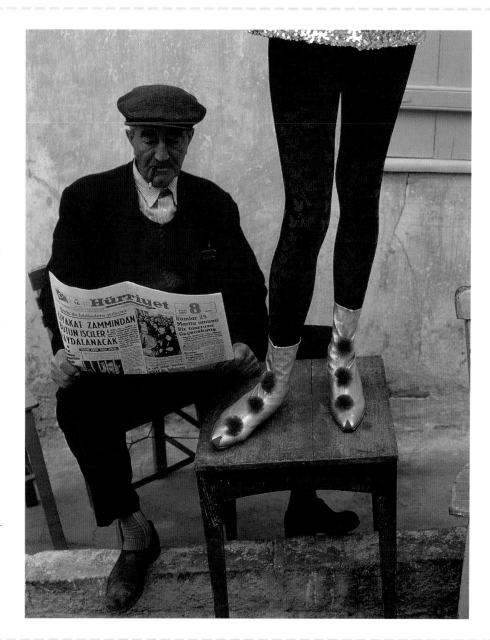

LEFT: This photograph shows the move from the contrived poses of earlier fashion images. The model's face has no importance, but the mix of legs in cheeky boots and an elderly man with his newspaper is amusing and eye-catching. Evins designed these short boots in 1965. The purple pom-poms and a cute, upturned toe, also purple, are matched with black and lilac tights made by Bonnie Doon.

LEFT: The Filipinos produced these wood wedgies in abundance, but being handmade, each showed variations in the "scene" carved into the heel. However, all showed the vernacular architecture and vegetation—small, deep-roofed houses and palm trees.

BELOW: This witty wedgie was made in the Philippines after World War II, and is testimony to the artistry of the craftsman who could not resist the opportunity to carve and paint the wood of the heel. It is missing the wide ribbon that once threaded through the loops at the heel to tie the sandal to the foot.

ABOVE: There were, of course, shortages of leather across war-torn Europe. But women were more concerned with fashion than shortages and Ferragamo's wedgies caused longing in every stylish heart, even copies made from alternative materials. This wedgie was made in Berlin and the heel is cork layered with plastic. The cover is suede but the straps are also plastic.

Ferragamo created his first wedgie in the late 1930s, but this style came into its own during the war. The wedge, a solid triangular sole that raises the back of the foot without the necessity of a separate heel, is easily constructed and can be made of wood or cork. Even under difficult conditions, shoe manufacturers could make the simple design and find the materials. Ferragamo refined the wedge by carving two sections of wood into "F" shapes that fitted together, giving the hard wedge flexibility.

LEFT: This shoe with a colorful print textile reveals the ingenuity of a designer working under difficult conditions. The cloth has been quilted to strengthen the cover, but this stitching also adds an interesting texture to the surface.

RIGHT: Pale, printed textile and a double ankle strap give this high-heeled sandal a cheerful air. The peep-toe is barred—perhaps an interesting comment on the British government's ban on peep-toes during the war.

Designers and manufacturers worked hard to make the wedgie smart and attractive, to give the basic materials an appearance that was more than merely ordinary, everyday footwear. Wooden wedges were painted to look like leather or covered with crocodile skin. The uppers were suede, braided plastic, and colored canvas. Ferragamo striped his wedge in three colors then added a coordinated patchwork cover. Gold braid was patterned onto suede vamps, or a canvas vamp was given a curly toe in homage to the Turkish slipper. He turned sandals, pumps, and boots into wedgies. Ferragamo also had a longing to create the "invisible" sandal and created a wedge covered in gold leather, then fixed rows of fishing lines over the toes and around the ankle.

LEFT: A young French woman gives a warm welcome to an American liberator in Paris. Pictures like this infuriated Englishwomen, not because they lacked handsome GIs, but because her gorgeous wedgies were not easily found in the dreary ration system imposed in England. The wedgies are an impressive copy of Ferragamo's original version.

Designers everywhere took their creative inspiration from Ferragamo. In Hawaii shoemakers carved palm-tree designs cut into the wooden wedge, while in France a circular hole was cut right through the wedge. The Chinese, meantime, covered the wedge with embroidered silk, and in California rubber was used to make a modest wedge with a striped canvas vamp, thus creating cheerful leisure or beachwear.

British women were told to stop worrying about nylons and to wear ankle socks or clumsy woolen stockings. Understandably they were not pleased to see photographs of French women after the Liberation of Paris in 1944. The French girls were snapped cycling through the city in pretty clothes and summery wedgies, yet life and clothes in London remained drab and regimented.

RIGHT: Ferragamo was endlessly inventive, not only with design but with material. During the lean war years, he used fishing line to make his "invisible shoes"—these elegant wedge sandals. Also, in a burst of inventiveness, he gave the wedge an unexpected curve.

The immediate post-war years were not a good time for any British industry that had not been directly related to the war effort. Besides, there was little incentive from a financially strapped market. Still, manufacturers such as H&R Rayne tried their best despite dreary government regulations. Every shoe had to bear a government stamp on its sole to show it met rationing restrictions—and ration coupons meant that women had no choice but to buy the things.

ABOVE: War shortages meant many manufacturers made dull shoes of conventional design. This heavy, practical style was, no doubt, widely worn but how women must have longed for something prettier, lighter, and more flattering.

LEFT: This plain oxford, with a low, wedged heel, depends for looks and style on the strongly colored markings of the snakeskin. Because the military did not use them, there was no shortage of reptile skins during the war, and this design has made the best of the situation.

ABOVE: Bata was proud to cater for the mass market, supplying stylish shoes to those on a stretched budget. These high heels with a short rounded toe were called Streamline, and their conventional but smart design guaranteed wide sales.

RIGHT: This moulded rubber Wellington boot was one of Bata's most popular boot styles, manufactured again and again between1950 and 1975. The mock astrakhan collar gave it a cosy appeal.

Bata

BELOW: These trainers with pink laces and sequined butterflies reveal the evolution, during the 1980s, of athletic footwear into glitzy fashion accessories. Trainers were, of course, comfortable and light and Bata responded to the demand for a pretty version that women could wear for dancing or arduous sightseeing holidays.

For many decades this company was world famous. In South Africa the name Bata was interchangeable with the word "shoe." But the Bata Shoe Company was unknown in the United States because, early in its history, it decided not to compete on the home turf of American manufacturers. Bata opened in Zin, in what is now the Czech Republic. After World War II, with its company headquarters now in London, Bata became the biggest shoe manufacturer in Europe, making everyday footwear at affordable prices. One of its biggest sellers was its white canvas plimsoll, or sneaker.

In 1964 the headquarters of Bata was again relocated, this time to Canada, but the influx of very cheap footwear from the Far East badly affected the company's sales. The business in Canada was closed in 2005, and Bata moved to Switzerland where it continues to retail its shoes as well as footwear from other manufacturers.

After the war European factories such as Bata were in poor shape, though the Marshall Plan, the American economic plan to revive Europe, was to prove effective in rebuilding manufacture. In the USA manufacturers were better placed and at last designers could return to their workbenches. The American designer David Evins re-launched his career, winning the Coty Award for shoe design in 1949.

In London rationing remained in force, but men and women were "clubbing" and dancing and determined to ignore the strictures of austerity. Once more Ferragamo came to the rescue by creating the platform shoe.

His first experiments involved thickening the wedge into a deep "platform" sole, then cutting a heel into the wedge. When the samba singer Carmen Miranda wore a pair on stage it caused a sensation. For her shoes Ferragamo covered the heel and the platform under the toes with gilded glass mosaics, while the vamp and ankle straps were of gold and black silk.

LEFT: In Spain, fishermen had long worn shoes, known as espadrilles, made of cork and raffia, or canvas. The style was modified in the '20s to make fashionable beach wear. This decorative sandal was a '40s variation, translating the traditional materials into a fashionable wedgie. Woven raffia makes the cover and, also, is layered over the heel.

Carmen's glass shoes wowed the crowd in 1938, and platforms became one of the most desired designs of the 1940s. Ferragamo made platforms of striped gold and silver, and gave the high heel a silver skin. He designed for clients such as Judy Garland and Indian Maharanis—a fairly exclusive market it must be said.

RIGHT: This glamorous shoe was inspired by Ferragamo's new platform design. Women loved his innovative thick sole and straight high heel. Lacking shiny rhinestones and crystals as decorative materials, this European black suede shoe has been cleverly decorated with metal studs.

ABOVE: During the war years, women found themselves working in jobs previously held by men. They went to munitions factories, delivered mail, and did farm work. For them, comfortable shoes were a priority, but a little dash of style was always welcome. The wedge heel, exaggerated tongue and mix of fabrics make this shoe interesting, although the fabrics are not of the highest quality. However it was a shoe that a golfer would be happy to wear on the greens.

In Hollywood platforms were studded with glittering rhinestones. The quality department store, Saks Fifth Avenue, displayed a pair of platform shoes that were ornamented with wavy lines of golden studs to emphasize the thickness of the platform. In Europe wooden-soled platforms were given raffia vamps, but for formal wear there were sassy suede-covered heels and platforms with ankle straps. Some had cut-out designs on the vamp, while others were cunningly punched with holes to overcome shortages in braid and dye.

RIGHT: By the 1940s, it had become perfectly respectable for women to play sport, and how Europeans must have yearned for the leisure to don excellent American tennis shoes, or sneakers and play a game or two. This photograph, taken in the U.S. during the '40s, presented a tantalising world of sun and peace.

Saks
Fifth Avenue

BELOW: This bronze, elegant court shoe, made for Saks Fifth Avenue, features fabric uppers and leather sole, and would look good worn at the office or for an evening out.

Saks Fifth Avenue is one of the most famous and most luxurious department stores in the world. In 1897 Andrew Saks opened a store in New York, then in 1923, merged with Gimbel Bros Inc. In 1924 Saks Fifth Avenue opened. The company opened branches in Florida, Chicago, and Beverly Hills and today has stores across the United States, Mexico, and the Middle East.

Saks Fifth Avenue has always supported the best in footwear, and through this policy shoe manufacturers and designers have had an outlet for innovative design, even during times of recession or war. This store stocks, among others, shoes by Gucci, Christian Louboutin, and Prada, and is proud to have served as a market for beginners and masters in the field of footwear. Any manufacturer or designer who is selected by Saks Fifth Avenue is assured of gaining a high reputation for quality and style.

ABOVE: These pretty vintage silver courts, with diamante decoration, are original Fenton Last shoes from Saks Fifth Avenue.

LEFT: Saks Fifth Avenue is the successor of a business founded by Andrew Saks in 1867, and incorporated in New York in 1902 as Saks & Company. This is an early view of the famous store on 5th Avenue in New York.

Shoemakers and women alike must have been grateful indeed for suede. It is made from poor quality leather, but the inside is brushed to give a velvety surface and flaws are not obvious. Suede can be easily dyed in various colors, and some of the prettiest shoes of the 1940s were made of it.

The '40s, though, was not a good decade for sportswomen. Alone at home with children to rear and war duties to perform, women had little time for gymnastics. Post-war rationing meant they continued to use wartime footwear. Army issue shoes were similar to the shoes men were wearing. Post-war German housewives were luckier in terms of comfort: they had access to Dr Martens' lace-up shoe with an air-impregnated sole. He began the manufacture of this ingenious design in 1947.

RIGHT: Dior's New Look, introduced while Europe was still reeling from the recent war, presented a look of high elegance and extravagance. Women, tired of make-do-and-mend wardrobes, were delighted by his vision.

BELOW: When Dior made it clear that court shoes were the correct footwear for his full skirts, the wedge and the platform fell quickly from favor. Court shoes with rounded toes flooded the European and American markets. A U.S. manufacturer produced this version.

In 1947 Dior presented his New Look, and the French abandoned the platform because Paris decreed that the high-heeled baby doll was the latest mode. Some had vinyl vamps, dotted with gold-colored spots, while others had a cut-away instep and a closed heel with an ankle strap. The ordinary women of Europe were hard pushed to find the yardage required by Dior's voluminous skirts. There were rumors that Dior was a sharp businessman who had found a way to bring wealthy Americans back to Paris, and that the New Look was designed only for them.

Perugia designed baby dolls but his versions hinted at erotic foot fetishism. The heel was very high and the foot appeared small, held as it was in short, round toes. But most baby dolls looked cute and simply sexy. As soon as they could fashionable women abandoned the wedgie, though manufacturers continued to produce them well into the early years of the next decade.

Actually most women were still struggling with post-war problems both on the domestic and public fronts. Shortages continued and money remained tight. Women resorted to buying black shoes, believing such footwear was inherently smart. They felt they could wear black during the day and through into the evening at the theater or a dinner party. The post-war years demanded such economies.

But women could always dream. Perhaps they dreamed of sequined scarlet pumps, the magical shoes worn by Judy Garland as she skipped down the Yellow Brick Road in *The Wizard of Oz*. Or else they fantasized about Ferragamo's frivolous gold wedgies, the velvety ankle straps held by gold chains—anything to distract them from the prevailing austerity.

LEFT: These are the ruby shoes worn by Dorothy, played by Judy Garland, in *The Wizard of Oz*, a hugely popular movie made in 1939. The sparkling, gorgeous shoes carried Dorothy to adventure and excitement, sadly lacking in the lives of the beleaguered housewives of Europe and Britain. Such magical footwear represented a happy world of dreamy escapism.

1950s
CHANGING DIRECTIONS

Paris reclaimed its domination of high fashion after the war. Christian Dior had caused widespread consternation when he produced his "New Look" just as the 1940s drew to a close, and thereafter the *haute couture* houses issued new silhouettes season after season. Full skirts became pencil skirts and tailored clothes over corseted waists and high bosoms were encouraged by French designers. Rationing continued in Britain though the government lifted the ban on peep-toes and allowed heels to exceed 2½ inches in height. But they continued to restrict the yardage allowed on clothing.

Perhaps wartime discipline and struggle encouraged a longing for smartness and elegance. Women followed every Parisian change in hemline, skirt shape, and of course shoe design. Fashion photographs from the early years of the decade show models in plain, short, round-toed baby dolls with sturdy high heels in leather or in front-lacing shoes with a low heel. For the mass market British designers made peep-toes and ankle straps, often in suede.

LEFT: High-heeled mules became a popular fashion choice after a technical advance made them much easier to wear than previous constructions. Here, the French movie star Brigitte Bardot, visits Rayne's, the Queen's shoe maker, in London's prestigious Bond Street, and seems pleased with the mules on offer.

ABOVE: The House of Dior was determined to show that dignity and elegance did not mean dull and conventional. Dior made these sky blue shoes and adorned them with a crossed loop of ribbon, trapped in a diamante buckle, to prove the point.

RIGHT: The heel was given great attention during the '50s, but it was not always the flesh version. The heel of the shoe was also given its due importance. Sir Edward Rayne created his famous Wedgwood heel when he translated the pottery company's much-loved porcelain motif to his shoes.

Shoes were not showy, though in Paris Perugia did not relinquish his old love of rich decoration. He ornamented evening shoes with buckles, made brocade covers, and dangled tassels from the vamp. *Vogue* presented a montage of Perugia designs from 1918 to 1956 and, without being told, it is difficult to date his luxurious designs.

The pump or court shoe dominated the high fashion look, and often reptile skin was used. The American manufacturer and retailer, Isaac Miller, was forward-looking. It commissioned Perugia and David Evins and both designers created excellent designs for all levels of the market. Evins was particularly prolific during the 1950s. In Paris Chanel re-opened her house and she too commissioned shoe designers. In 1959 Massaro

designed the famous Chanel cream pumps with black toe and heel, a style that persists to this day.

Manufacturers overcame ongoing shortages by giving significance to the heel. Rhinestones, crystals, or stripes covered the high heels of this decade, and not only in Hollywood. The British manufacturer Raynes used motifs taken from much-loved traditional Wedgwood porcelain. He also used confetti-colored plastic, carved wood, and satin on his heels. In America one designer stacked little crystal baubles to make a heel, while another made the heel in a different pattern from the vamp. David Evins experimented with decorative heels but he did not neglect the rest of the shoe and produced a quilted cover on one of his creations.

LEFT: The inventive approach to decorative heels is displayed in this array from the Northampton Museum, England. Floral motifs, fish scales, Grecian ornament, or Chinese dragons indicate designers drew inspiration from many sources to enhance this small, narrow but exciting part of women's footwear.

Teenagers and young women tended to ignore Paris as a fashion source: Hollywood films were their inspiration. They preferred the full skirts or the daring blue jeans worn by youthful American stars. And American girls developed a passion for sneakers and spectator shoes worn with ankle socks; these young women were known as "bobby-soxers." The sneakers came in patterned canvas and had a longer toe than earlier versions. The spectators had crepe rubber soles, and generally, dark leather trimmed only the latchet and tongue, and not the toe-cap, as in previous designs.

ABOVE: U.S. teenagers were allowed freedoms unknown before the war. Young girls were permitted to play sport, drive, and go out in the evening, without escorts, to enjoy the frenzy of rock 'n' roll music. All these developments may account for the popularity among girls for boyish, easy-to-wear spectator shoes which they wore with childish ankle socks.

RIGHT: The box advertises the product as suitable for "All Court Games" and having molded soles, but sneakers or plimsolls became favorite all-day footwear among adolescent boys and girls. Made of canvas, the shoes can be worn without socks and are sturdy and comfortable.

The bobby-sox craze was attributed to rock 'n' roll and jive. This dance involved a complex set of steps and pirouettes, and the girls were lifted and whirled about the floor. However, the name was first given to the young women who mobbed popular singers such as Frank Sinatra and Dean Martin. The widespread use of the gramophone took American popular music to the world. Chuck Berry, Fats Domino, and Elvis Presley inspired the young, and Elvis especially helped make the wild dance moves of jive very popular. His blue suede crepe-soled shoes and the low-heeled shoes of the bobby-soxers set the pace.

LEFT: Popular music changed considerably in the '50s. Rock 'n' rollers—Elvis Presley, Little Richard, and the like, overcame the crooners, such as Frank Sinatra and Dean Martin. Adolescents matched their dance movements to the insistent rhythm of the new sound. Young men and women alike wore sneakers, and other sports shoes as they threw themselves around the dance floor.

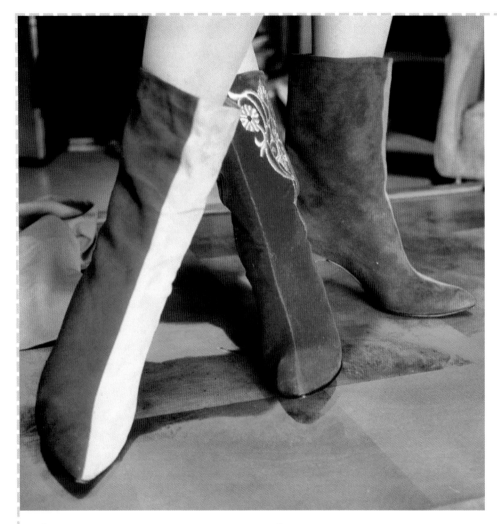

ABOVE: These calf-length boots are testimony to Beth Levine's unflagging creativity and originality. She was not afraid to mix blue and beige in suede, or embroider red velvet with gold Moroccan embroidery. On the third boot, on the right, she made a boot that was half blue, and half orange. Her daring was appreciated by many women, and in the 1960s, the Herbert Levine Company concentrated on the 'sportive' look and was the leader in what became a major trend for fashion boots.

RIGHT: In the 1950s, the Herbert Levine Company invented the Spring-O-Later, making mules easier to wear, and the 'stocking boot' in which Beth found a way of attaching the shoe to the stocking. These mules are attached to textured black stockings, described at the time as 'nylon net opera length hose.'

The Herbert
Levine
Company

In 1948, Beth and Herbert Levine opened their own shoe company in Manhattan, New York. Beth was the designer, although the shoes were marketed under the company name (her husband's name). Her great strength lay in anticipating forthcoming fashions, and she he was innovative, even daring in her approach. Under her direction, the company produced Spring-O-Laters, and stocking boots. The fashion boot was popularised by the Herbert Levine Company in the 60s, and Beth created footwear in new synthetic fabrics, such as vinyl and acrylic. A pair of sandals was bedecked with inner soles of Astroturf; another pair was fabricated from plaited sweetie wrappers. Her Kabuki was an aerodynamic design, with a curved flat attachment fitted to the sole under the instep. Its appearance was too odd to attract many buyers. Faced by foreign imports and an increasingly competitive home market, the Herbert Levine Company closed in 1975

LEFT: Beth Levine adds details to bring distinction to a court shoe. The long toe is very slightly blunted, and enclosed in a shiny fabric that contrasts with the matt upper. A small circular jewel softens the space between the straight line of the toe fabric and the straight cut of the vamp.

BELOW: The smooth shiny fabric of the toe is repeated on the heel. The shape of the stiletto, too, expresses Levine's quirky design sense. It is deeply waisted but the curve is lower than usual, falling as it does close to the heel tip.

Another youthful fashion was that of flat ballerina pumps. These suited full-gathered skirts and petticoats but were also perfect when combined with narrow "cigarette" or Capri pants. The designer Claire McCardell had suggested putting a hard sole on the soft-soled ballet shoe to the American manufacturer Capezio in 1941. They were built on dance shoe lasts and sold well, but the style only became a best-seller in the 1950s after the French movie star and blonde pinup Brigitte Bardot requested a small French shoemaker, Rose Repetto, to create a pair for her to wear in the movie *And God Created Woman* (1956). Her *cendrillons* or ballet shoes were red but that timeless fashion icon, Audrey Hepburn, sported a pair of green velvet *cendrillons*. Ballet shoes have been on sale ever since, enjoying a big revival in the early twenty-first century.

LEFT: Shortages of leather continued to affect British shoe manufacturers. This shoe shows the ingenuity of the makers. It mixes suede and a lace textile, touched up with a ribbon threaded round the throat to create stylish footwear.

ABOVE: In reaction to the difficult fashion years of the '40s, Paris ruled that women should strive for a dignified elegance. This shoe epitomizes the understated luxury of quality manufacture, modest style, and polished lizard skin. The new shape overtook the sexy heels and small, round toes of the briefly popular baby doll style.

LEFT: Dior's New Look decided conventional court shoes were the correct accessories for the style. Debenhams (the English department store), shoe slipped past the dull rule by applying a brilliant color to a quality round-toed, high-heeled court shoe.

Roger Vivier is credited with designing the first stiletto heel, a high needle construction, reinforced with steel to prevent it snapping. It was named after the thin but deadly Italian dagger. The appeal of these sexy shoes crossed the generations. Marilyn Monroe sashayed around in naughty red sequin-sparkled stilettos. Dior made a pair with gypsy lacing up the center of the vamp, and for the mass market H.R. Rayne covered a pair in rhinestones.

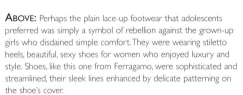

ABOVE: Perhaps the plain lace-up footwear that adolescents preferred was simply a symbol of rebellion against the grown-up girls who disdained simple comfort. They were wearing stiletto heels, beautiful, sexy shoes for women who enjoyed luxury and style. Shoes, like this one from Ferragamo, were sophisticated and streamlined, their sleek lines enhanced by delicate patterning on the shoe's cover.

BELOW: Lace was a major trend in footwear. The textile was advertised as a kind of healthy Airtex because it allowed the foot to breath, but few women cared about that. They adored the lacy effect. Combined with shiny patent leather and set on stiletto heels, the lace made for a stunning design. The winkle picker toe is emphasized by a cap of patent leather.

The wearing of stilettos was banned in various buildings because they pockmarked the floors, but women loved them despite dire warnings from health experts about the destructive effect on feet and posture. Such thin high heels caused the legs to look longer and shapelier than they were, while emphasizing buttocks and bust. The vamp was long and cut low at the toes. The stiletto heel made for a seriously sexy shoe.

The mule returned once more in the late 1950s. The American designer Beth Levine was shown an innovation that placed an elastic tape on the inner sole, bridging the space between the ball and the heel of the foot. As the tape kept the foot on the shoe, the inventor intended them for orthopedic use. Levine, though, used the elastic in a high heel mule.

BELOW: This wedgie mule looks like a bedroom slipper, but the leopard skin print ensured it would not look amiss if worn wandering the deck of a liner, or during an air flight. The Hollywood manufacturer described it as a "leisure" mule.

She called her samples Spring-O-Laters and they sold out of the stores within days in Chicago and Los Angeles. The market was soon flooded with Spring-O-Laters, partly because the invention was never patented and manufacturers were able to rush copies to the market without any red tape to hinder them.

These mules were high heeled and intended for outdoor wear as indicated in their use of leather, textile, vinyl, plastic, and Plexiglas. Bright colors in vinyl were matched with patterned Plexiglas heels, while another sample sported colorful checkered brocade. These Spring-O-Laters were popular throughout the 1950s.

BELOW: The mule has long been associated with the boudoir, and even now, in the United States, mules, adorned with marabou or stork feathers, still sell well as indoor or bedroom wear. The American marabou mule is a sexy piece of footwear showing, as it does, the naked foot resting on a high heel, its toes partially hidden by a fluffy feathered covering. Marilyn Monroe wore them to great effect in *The Seven Year Itch*.

LEFT: Capezio called this sandal the Baby Louise, and he wanted the design to enhance a tanned foot. Also, he intended that his graceful use of straps would allow the wearer to feel elegant whether she wore the sandals for day or evening wear. The Cuban heel is low enough to be comfortable walking but suited also to dancing.

BELOW: Capezio uses his distinctive signature as the company logo. It appears in shop displays and is stamped in his footwear. This black sandal is designed for dancing. The company built its reputation on dance shoes, but has extended its range and also manufactures high fashion footwear.

Capezio

LEFT: This view of the black sandal (see previous page) shows straps that cross over the front before being closed by a buckle. It is a design that flatters the ankle. The heel is a medium high Cuban shape, and Capezio made this footwear to be worn as a Latin American dance shoe.

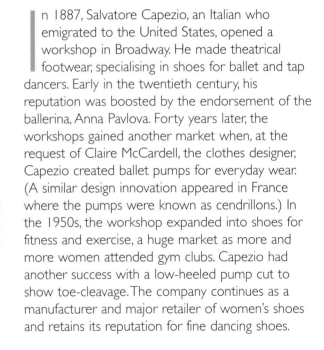

In 1887, Salvatore Capezio, an Italian who emigrated to the United States, opened a workshop in Broadway. He made theatrical footwear, specialising in shoes for ballet and tap dancers. Early in the twentieth century, his reputation was boosted by the endorsement of the ballerina, Anna Pavlova. Forty years later, the workshops gained another market when, at the request of Claire McCardell, the clothes designer, Capezio created ballet pumps for everyday wear. (A similar design innovation appeared in France where the pumps were known as cendrillons.) In the 1950s, the workshop expanded into shoes for fitness and exercise, a huge market as more and more women attended gym clubs. Capezio had another success with a low-heeled pump cut to show toe-cleavage. The company continues as a manufacturer and major retailer of women's shoes and retains its reputation for fine dancing shoes.

LEFT: The sleek lines of this shoe belie its practical purpose. It is closefitting to support the foot, strapped to stay on the foot, and the sole reveals the metal fittings required for tap dancing.

ABOVE: The Spring-O-Later was not used by this Italian manufacturer. He relied on gaily colored plastic strips to give his wooden mules selling appeal. Zigzag stitching and a tiny buckle, all colored gold, add a little pizzazz to the sandal.

LEFT: These wooden mules are made in Vietnam. An Oriental style of decorative floral motifs is used to charming effect. The soles are patterned in black and white but a colorful, sequined butterfly sits on the vamp. Any review of the story of mule sandals shows their appeal is worldwide, demonstrating the inherent sex appeal of these "half shoes."

Designers created the cantilevered shoe on which the mid-sole was raised by a piece of metal curving between arch and toes. This was strong enough to balance the foot without the need of a heel. The heelless shoe was a dream—a real challenge for designers in the 1950s—and various solutions were offered to the market. Beth Levine designed her "floating" shoe, the Kabuki. However, these experiments were seen as novelties and did not sell widely.

Roland Jourdan, who had taken over his father's workshop, brought relief to women suffering in high mules and stilettos. He revamped the pump with an elongated toe and set the heel back on the sole, but it was a comfortable low heel. He decorated the cover with buckles, thus drawing attention away from the heel. Another designer, Margaret Jerrold, followed his shape, though her heels were given a quirky, slightly bulged heel.

Sport and exercise returned to the agenda. White canvas tennis shoes, sneakers, were always used on the tennis court and their use was extended to the athletics track. In the 1956 Olympics, American and Australian women dominated the women's track events. Skiing came into vogue and women were going on ski holidays. Again, they turned to the sturdy designs made for men, and front-lacing ankle boots were useful.

LEFT: Charles Jourdan contributed to the fashionable interest in the heel of the foot with this sling-back. This red satin creation, touched up with a glitzy buckle, creates a fine evening shoe.

Golf was increasingly popular, especially after the Women's Championships started in 1946. Mrs Zaharias, an American player, was championship winner throughout the 1950s. Golfing footwear assumed a style that for many years was to remain a convention: spiked soles, so as not to ruin the golfing green, showy fringed tongues, and two pairs of eyelets. Essentially they were modified copies of the two-tone, spectator or co-respondent shoe. To complete the look lady players wore ankle socks with their golfing shoes.

The thousands of passengers who traveled on the great liners that sailed from Europe to New York, Cape Town, and Sydney needed casual shoes. During these long sea journeys, deck sports whiled away the time. Sneakers and sandals—the vamps cut out rather than strapped—with rubber or crepe soles and firmly buckled straps proved useful, and these came in the bright cheerful colors of canvas.

RIGHT: A close look shows that the women in the crowd are wearing spectators or oxfords. The champion golfer, Babe Didrickson Zacharias, seems to be in a pair of flexible sports shoes of the kind made by Adidas in the '50s. Golf was increasingly popular as a sport among American and English women, and here Babe is competing in a charity match for the American Women's Volunteer Services.

LEFT: The Americans devised a method of stitching together all the elements of a fabric sandal before inserting a platform and attaching a heel. The construction required little skill and inexpensive textiles were used. The sandals, often known as California casuals, were popular for summer and vacation weather, but lost their attraction as wedge heels fell out of fashion.

LEFT: Raymond Massaro is the grandson of Sébastien, the founder of the family firm. Raymond modernized the firm but he has never abandoned his commitment to the craft of the cordwainer. He is proud to be photographed, surrounded by the wooden lasts and innumerable shoes and boots created in the Massaro workshops.

BELOW: A narrow line of silver around the throat gives a distinctive touch to these quiet black court shoes. They were made in the mid-twentieth century and the maker's name is stamped in the interior, as are heraldic symbols indicating that Massaro was the appointed shoemaker of noble clients.

Massaro

Sébastien Massaro opened his shoemaking business in the rue de la Paix, Paris, in 1894 and in due course trained his four sons as cordwainers. Small and elite, the family business crafted bespoke footwear for a select group of loyal customers.

The workshop only reached a wider market under the direction of the founder's grandson, Raymond. He was born in 1929 and was almost thirty years old when he designed for Coco Chanel, creating a two-tone pump that has never been out of production: the sling-back version proved equally popular. He worked in liaison with Chanel for some years. Raymond Massaro maintained the high craftsmanship of his family, and went on to design for many couturiers and clothes designers. In 1994 he was awarded the title Master of Art by the French government in recognition of his work.

RIGHT: Massaro gained wide public recognition after he designed his very successful two-tone Chanel pumps in 1957. He has become a favored designer among the rich and famous, even earning the title "Bootmaker to The Stars." This fame gave him licence to create wild designs, such as these witty platforms propped up by skipping, golden legs.

On cruises, formal captains' dinners and dancing filled the evenings, so women travelers packed their pumps and high heeled shoes. Peep toes and ankle straps were pretty and much liked as dance footwear. One American manufacturer put a double row of faux pearls on his ankle strap, while British shoes continued to be a mix of suede and leather, revealing that some shortages had not yet been overcome.

BELOW: Pink lace is used to create a teasing, semi-naked shoe although the toe is covered with an inner reinforcement. The heels, of medium height, are set close to the shank. This was a charming day shoe for summer.

Air travel was very expensive and there were few long-haul flights. A trip from London to Cape Town, for instance, could only be achieved with numerous stops down the length of Africa. It was perceived as a smart event, and women passengers dressed in tailored suits and high-heeled shoes. These were usually closed court shoe style: there was a widespread belief that these were hardier than ankle straps and peep toes. Some women carried slippers or ballet shoes to wear on the flight.

American and European women enjoyed the choice of shoes more than those in rationed Britain. For much of the 1950s, British women continued to wear "demob" shoes, front laced with five pairs of eyelets. Britain acquired an enviable reputation for classic, plain court shoes in fine leathers, but sales were largely confined to the high end of the market.

LEFT: Black shoes were bought more than any other color because women believed black would carry them from day to evening wear without necessitating a change of shoes. These sling-backs are delightful dance shoes, enhanced by a peep toe. But they have a subtle brogue trim on the throat and toe, and this gives them a daytime mood.

LEFT: The court shoe, with an uncluttered vamp and a high heel, had steady sales throughout the '50s, proving shoppers were cautious in their fashion purchases. This modest leather winklepicker has an unobtrusive self-fabric ornament on the vamp, and the style is typical of the conventional taste of most women.

ABOVE: Footwear, exhibitionist, glitzy, and flamboyant, had a market, although perhaps not at the same level as conventional footwear. But there must have been an elbow fight for these mules. The unexpected partnership of metal and wood, the elegant profile of the sole, and the extravagant use of silver sequins have all been mixed to create a pair of fabulous mules.

The United States continued to be the major manufacturer and innovator, and Florsheim continued to cater for that nation. Italian designers were emerging as major players in footwear, exploiting a long tradition of craftsmanship. Elsewhere Portugal and Brazil were producing small manufacturers, as were Japan and Germany. But the Hollywood style, whether tomboyish, glamorous or dignified, continued to influence taste everywhere.

There were great improvements in the comfort, fit and purpose of footwear. Men, women, and children benefited, and the needs of athletes were given much thought. Fabrics were improved while new ones were developed. The 1950s liked its court shoes, its stilettos, and its little velvet pumps, but teenage demand was to cause major changes in the market.

BELOW: Ferragamo gave women elegant designs that could be worn with a business outfit, or a tweed, or silk skirt. He gave them shoes that were more suited to an active working life than stilettos or winklepickers. But the long vamp, the blunted toe, and subtle color of his low-heeled shoe could never be accused of having a frumpy comfort.

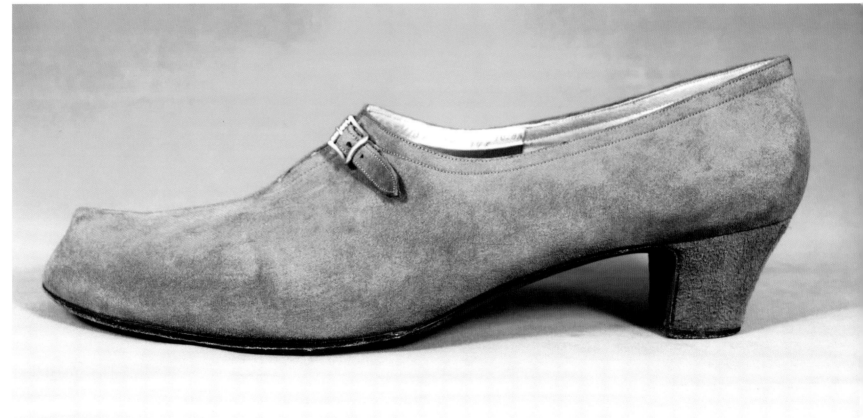

1960s
LOAFERS AND LIBERATION

After World War II, the birth rate shot up in western societies. By the 1960s these children, the so-called "baby boomers," had become young grown-ups who now formed the majority of the population. As a generation they were rebellious, and their rebellion was voiced by rock music in particular. Wherever rock and folk musicians performed—in tents, outdoor venues, or small clubs—they attracted audiences eager to hear their songs of anger and protest. And the young women in the audience did not "dress" for the occasion: they did not put on cocktail dresses, as their mothers might have done, but wore jeans and T-shirts. Their footwear reflected this unconventional approach to dress. They wore sandals and low-heeled pumps, while the most rebellious donned men's work boots.

LEFT: The '60s generation found their rebellious feelings were expressed by young musicians, who wrote songs of protest against the established authorities and social conventions. The singer, Joan Baez, and Bob Dylan, poet and musician, were among the leading performers of this movement, and both attracted huge youthful audiences.

Shoemakers picked up on the social changes. Beth Levine produced a low-heeled sandal with a single thin strap running from the big toe to the ankle strap, while Pierre Cardin made low-heeled square-toed boots. In 1963 an American manufacturer advertised his so-called "devilish look." His illustrations showed calf-high boots in red suede and shiny leather.

BELOW: Established designers picked up on the preference for sandals prevalent among young women. But high-end manufacturers tended to make pretty versions, not entirely suitable for protest meetings. This Italian designer arranged delicate straps, threaded through a triangle over the arch and then tied around the ankle.

ABOVE: A small detail can change a design from pretty to special, as demonstrated by the gold-tipped Louis heel on this sandal.

The stiletto heel, such a favorite in the 1950s, did not survive for long, especially when it was combined with a long, pointed toe. The British called the new style "the winkle picker." This footwear was favored by an elaborately dressed group of young people known as the Mods. But even for them the winkle picker proved too uncomfortable, and the fashion was short-lived.

In the U.S. the Civil Rights Movement, the African-American struggle for equality, was also supported by many young white Americans. It fueled the mood of rejection of old values. In Britain the class system provoked anger and the young rebelled against the Establishment. Across the Channel, French students demanded changes in their rigid educational and social systems.

BELOW: Freeman Hardy Willis of England retailed this shoe. The winklepicker has a cover of Lurex. The throat is elasticized at the vamp throat to ensure the Lurex textile, a comparatively soft fabric, sits firmly on the foot.

RIGHT: Italian craftsmen continued to make footwear suited to smart dressing, or for commissions from *haut couture* houses. This footwear ignores any youthful protest movement. This shoe is a high quality product: an open-weave cover surrounds the winklepicker toe to form a cage that allows tantalising glimpses of the toe cleavage and the arch of the foot.

Were radical young women interested in the style of haughty Parisian couture houses? No, they preferred the relaxed American style and gingham check dresses that Brigitte Bardot sported, or admired the "art student" look of jeans, long sweaters, and low-heeled pumps.

However, it was the couturier Yves Saint Laurent who designed the Pilgrim pump with a buckle on the vamp. The toe was blunt but rounded and the heel was low. The original square buckle was transformed into a circle or a rhinestone-dotted oval. In Britain H&R Rayne produced pumps, making satin evening versions decorated with buckles or rows of diamante.

BELOW: This shoe represents the exciting possibilities of design brought by a technology that found new efficient ways of using textiles. A Scots plaid fabric is allied with black plastic. The toe is long and narrow and the shoe has a fashionably low Louis heel. This height complemented the short skirts of the time.

BELOW: Bruno Magli may not be known for innovative design but, nevertheless, his shoes are easily recognizable. Shoppers can rely on his use of the best leather and the craftsmanship of his production. Subtle details, such as the small triangular gap on the vamp, also identify a Magli shoe.

Bruno
Magli

This Italian company began life in the 1930s as a manufacturer of conventional footwear. However, when the founder's nephew Morris Magli became the company's president in the 1960s there was a growing recognition of Italian craftsmen and the high quality of their work. His wife, Rita, became the company's creative director and was responsible for modernizing the company. Bruno Magli made franchise arrangements with shoe manufacturers around the world.

In the 1990s the creative talents of Rolf Grueterich and the founder's granddaughter, also called Rita, combined to give the company a global identity as a high-end manufacturer. Bruno Magli expanded into leather clothes, gloves, and other accessories. Its distinctive theme was the production of matching shoes and purses. The Magli family lost overall control of the company when the Opera organisation bought majority shares in the 1990s.

ABOVE: The beautiful simplicity of this classic court shoe needs no decoration. It relies on the gleam and texture of polished reptile skin for its appeal. The heel curves into the shank which is balanced by a long toe. Magli designed it in 1960.

RIGHT: This shoe has all the characteristics of Bruno Magli's work —fine leather, purity of design, and a dignified decorative detail. His quality footwear is made for the high end of the market.

SHOES   The Ultimate Accessory

During the 1950s an exclusive New York retailer began to import handcrafted casual shoes from Belgium. They were designed on the pattern of a Belgian peasant slipper, had low heels and stitched oval-shaped vamps decorated with small bows. They became known as loafers, and by the 1960s they were much copied and very popular for their comfort and elegance.

The trend to sexual liberation was symbolized by the mini skirt, a fashion defying all traditional conventions of feminine modesty. It provoked the "Dolly Bird" look as personified by the slender young English model, Twiggy. The image called for childlike shoes and—as little girls were conventionally shod in Baby Janes—round-toed shoes with a buttoned cross bar. André Courrèges marketed an adult version of the Mary Jane.

RIGHT: Twiggy epitomized the girlish Dolly Bird look of the '60s. Here, she has rejected any coiffure and instead, her hair is pulled up in two schoolgirl bunches. She wears a variation of Baby Jane shoes, a style that, for generations, had been confined to small female children under the age of ten.

LEFT: Charles Jordan constructed a neat silhouette of blunt toe and short blunt heel. He continued the symmetry through a repetitive use of transparent acrylic—in a medal on the vamp and on the lower half of the heel.

Mary Quant, who employed the shoe designer Walter Steiger, commissioned Twiggy to be photographed in what looked like tap dancer's footwear. These black patent shoes were girlish in appearance and tied with white ribbons.

LEFT: The synthetic fabric, PVC, with its gleaming surface was completely modern, capturing the smooth functional look of the machinery of space exploration. Mary Quant used it extensively: she made this sleek shoe with its deep vamp. The style was known in the U.S. as the "pant boot" because it looked so well with the pantsuits, or trouser suits, popular in the '60s.

ABOVE: This rainboot is constructed from machine-molded plastic and makes the zip fastener into a blatant design statement. Through her use of synthetic fabrics and minimalist design, Mary Quant's footwear was a determined expression of modernity. Here, a gold colored heel is an unexpected addition to the black of the boot and both have a smooth, plastic surface.

RIGHT: Mary Quant, the British fashion designer, is shown launching her range of boots and shoes, called Quant Afoot. She is sitting on the floor surrounded by models flaunting her footwear.

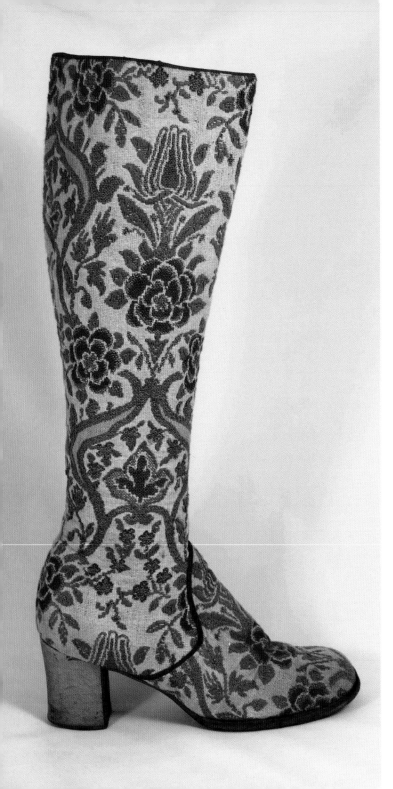

LEFT: This boot came from Chelsea Cobblers, an English boutique footwear company. Although the pattern is European, the embroidery carries the ethnic, handcrafted appearance favored by a generation interested in the cultures of non-industrial countries.

BELOW: The close fit and soft cover are typical of the "Go-Go" boot, first conceived by the French designer André Courrèges and copied by many others. This silver version comes from Jeunesse, and reflects the contemporary love of the "Space Age" look, provoked by the space explorations of the time.

She also used the glossy qualities of synthetic PVC and created straight, shiny boots with a squared toe: an exposed zip ran up the outside leg. On one of her designs, the top length of the boot could be removed, leaving a shoe in its place. Her footwear was a slick statement of modernity.

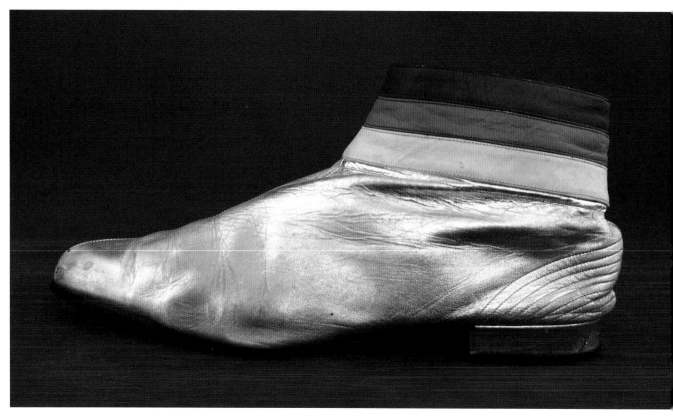

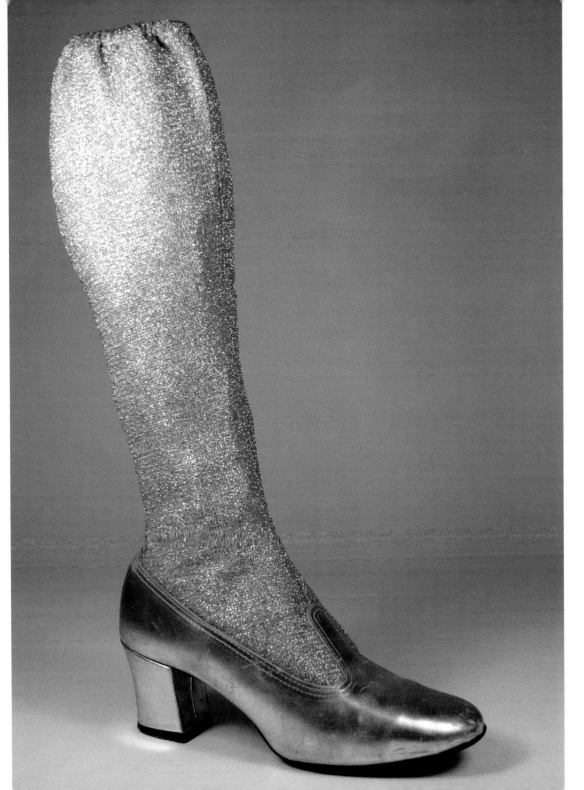

The British rock bands, The Beatles and The Rolling Stones, echoed the success of Twiggy, a young working class woman. These musicians were also outside the rigidities of the British class system. Although the cause of the defiance of British youth was not as obvious as the racial and gender debates in the USA, the anti-Establishment movement was of great significance to society in Great Britain.

The girls of the 1960s were busy going on demonstrations against university authorities or marching for nuclear disarmament, or dancing at exuberant music festivals. They wanted informal clothes and the boot proved the best footwear for the casual style of the decade.

LEFT: Beth Levine received the prestigious fashion Coty Award in 1967 for her stocking boot, as well as her stretch boots. Her work provoked many imitations such as this silver pump, transformed into a knee-high boot when silver stretch Lurex was attached to the shoe. An elastic seam at the throat of the Lurex ensures the boot will not droop.

BELOW: Steiger finishes his classic court shoe with a gleaming metallic toe, adding a subtle dash to the conventional style, but the heel is used to make a more emphatic statement.

RIGHT: The highly polished metallic heel swoops as high as the heel counter, and acts as a mirror reflecting light and shadow. This design confirms Steiger has a designer who never fails to produce glamorous footwear.

Walter
Steiger

LEFT: Sex appeal, the design signature of Walter Steger, is unmistakeable in this peeptoe sandal, its very high heel held on by a skimpy strap twisted round the ankle.

BELOW: Steiger was, of course, intrigued by the possibilities of leather. He gave these sandals a closely woven leather vamp and then lifted the dense appearance of the weave by adding a narrow slingback strap.

Walter Steiger was taught the craft of cordwainer by his family in Geneva, Switzerland, and worked for Bally, the major Swiss shoe manufacturer. Mary Quant employed him as a designer in 1960s London before Steiger moved to Paris in 1973. He opened a workshop and was commissioned by Chanel, Nina Ricci, Chloe and other leading fashion houses. Nowadays, Walter Steiger designs and crafts his products in Italy. His shoes are elegant, brilliantly coloured and strikingly patterned (for instance he produced pumps dotted with giant polka dots). Steiger has 25 showcase retail outlets in high-end shopping districts around the world, and the boutique interiors are sleek and luxurious. His work realises high sales and his early designs have become vintage collectables.

In 1964 the French designer André Courrèges put his models in low-heeled white plastic boots adorned with a clear cut-out slot near the top. Or models went down the catwalk in shiny plastic close-fitting ankle boots with a zipper fitting. These became known as "go-go boots" and they could be worn anywhere, even on the dance floor. Other manufacturers were quick to bring out their own versions.

RIGHT: In the dizzy world of fashion, stocking boots and bright patterning prevailed but shoppers also needed more sensible footwear. These boots have an interesting dipped throat and a line of saddle stitching, they are weatherproof but smart, and this demure style of boot sold well.

Yves Saint Laurent made long plastic boots patterned with squares of hard color in homage to the abstract Dutch painter, Piet Mondrian. David Evins presented a leopard skin boot while another American designer produced a wedgie boot. Over-the-knee boots made to look like fishnet tights and furnished with a Plexiglas heel came from Beth and Herbert Levine. Still another U.S. manufacturer produced stretch-vinyl high boots in faux patchwork of animal prints.

RIGHT: During the '60s, one section of the market loved glitter and intricate traditional design, but others preferred modernity and geometric lines. In 1968, Pierre Cardin, the couture French designer, presented these outfits of narrow silhouettes, marked by abstract shapes of color, and accessorized with close-fitting thigh-high boots and long gloves.

It was Barbara Hulanicki, founder of the famous London boutique Biba, who made the most popular version of the 1960s boot. Her long skin-tight boot with a medium heel came in a range of fabrics and party colors and sold by the thousand.

ABOVE: Clog sandals were hardwearing and organic but early versions tended towards a heavy, sometimes clumsy, appearance. This pair is shaped and curved, while the raffia weave and open toe make feminine, cheerful summer wear.

LEFT: These sandals were made for women who were not very interested in style but the color mix on the thick straps give these sturdy sandals some visual appeal. The spaced rubber pads on the sole make an unobtrusive, but interestingly ridged line.

But beyond the dolly birds of London fashion, there was of course another mood in the 1960s. It started in the U.S. where a growing number of people were alarmed by the rapid industrialization of the western world. Fears of pollution from the chemical waste of the huge factories, and the pesticides used in agriculture, drove these people to an alternative way of living. They called for a return to organic farming methods and natural materials.

Groups took to living in communes where they could grow their own food. They wore only cotton and wool, and the women wandered round in long peasant dresses and sandals. Some were restless, even nomadic, and hitched or drove camper vans and motor bikes, refusing to settle into respectability. American musicians voiced the ideals of these people, the hippies, and sang protest songs against the commercialization of American life. The men grew beards and women had long unstyled hair.

BELOW: In 1964, Karl Birkenstock presented his flexible arch support, claiming it molded itself to the individual's foot shape. Ever since, the cork footbed and chunky straps of his sandal have had steady sales. The Birkenstock came in a variety of styles this, with a single narrow strap, is the Madrid range.

RIGHT: Even when Rayne made a range of government Utility shoes during the war, the company was committed to quality and design. The distribution of jeweled studs on the throat and stiletto heel are a masterly touch on this classic court shoe.

BELOW: The netted cut-outs, spread like a fan across the vamp, are proof of the inventive creativity of Rayne. The straight sturdy heel and ankle strap make this a beautiful dancing shoe, or actually one suited to any evening event.

H&R
Rayne

Henry Ryan opened Rayne, a theatrical costumier in London, in the 1880s. When his son took over, the company concentrated on footwear. In 1920 a shop was opened on Bond Street along with a factory in North London. In the 1930s H&R Rayne, as the company was now known, won a contract with the American company Delman, and this was maintained even after Delman changed ownership in the 1950s. H&R Rayne was commissioned to make shoes for Roger Vivier, Mary Quant, and Hardy Amies.

The founder's grandson, Edward Rayne, was devoted to the family business and became an important figure in British shoe manufacture, fighting for the industry at every turn. However, H&R Rayne, like other established shoemakers on both sides of the Atlantic, was blind to commercial change. First, Italian craftsmen made inroads on the market, then imports came from the Far East. H&R Rayne struggled on under various buy-out deals, but finally closed in 1994.

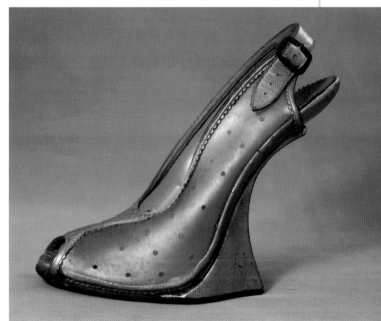

LEFT: The stamps inside this Rayne shoe include the heraldic symbol of the British monarchy to advertise royal patronage of the company. This 1950s shoe, with a diamante buckle that seemingly gathers up the vamp to reveal the toes, is one of Rayne's many charming designs.

ABOVE: Perhaps war shortages goaded Rayne into designing a heelless shoe, or perhaps this design represented a challenge. Rayne made it in the 1940s and, during the 1950s, numerous others continued to explore the construction. However, this design has never had popular appeal.

The movement inspired the German company Birkenstock to engineer a new kind of sandal. Fashioned on ergonomic principles, it mimicked the contours of the foot. The sole was constructed from a mix of jute, cork, and natural latex and was designed to improve circulation and allow the toes to spread in a natural way. Two thick leather bands with large buckles held this wonder sole to the foot. It was described as the ugliest footwear in the world, but since its inception it has remained a best-seller. Birkenstock have produced forty-six variations, while many other manufacturers have copied the clunky design.

RIGHT: Western fashion during the '60s embraced the glitter and sequins used extensively in India and Arabic countries. The apparent simplicity of this Baby Jane is contradicted by a heel richly decorated with sparkling rhinestone and metal.

BELOW: This is a variation of the Baby Jane shoe, and retains the easy round toe and bar strap. The thick heel complements the child-like appearance: a stiletto would have a very different effect.

In Brazil a company produced a rubber and plastic version of the world's earliest footwear, the thong sandal. New Zealanders claimed they made the rubber style first, calling them "jandals," but the Brazilian product had bigger sales and the sandals quickly came to be known everywhere as flip-flops.

The young mini-skirted women who rocked to the sound of The Beatles and The Rolling Stones were not so keen on natural or basic unadorned footwear. Biba's round-toed pumps with their thick low heels, cross bars, or ankle straps were considered much more stylish. These were often made in suede and came in many colors.

However, the long skirts of the hippies were, inevitably, absorbed by the fashion world. *Vogue* featured women in billowing kaftans, preferably bought in Morocco or India. Glittery gold-colored sandals, or satin pumps encrusted with crystals or rhinestones were chosen to go with these vibrant "ethnic" garments. Fabric loafers in colorful patterns also suited the relaxed, loose look of the caftan.

RIGHT: This shimmering silver shoe was designed for evening wear and the new maxi skirt. Its sumptuous decoration satisfied the fashionable lust for sequins and beads.

LEFT: Ballin, Italy is stamped on this shoe, made to appeal to a wide market. The shape was fashionable, but the winklepicker does not seem uncomfortable when allied with a Louis heel. The navy leather is cut out; the cord threaded through the loops is white plastic vitello.

BELOW: The market for sophisticated footwear may have shrunk but it did not disappear in the '60s. Older women would choose this classic high-heeled court shoe in pink satin for formal wear, such as a wedding, the opera, or an evening event.

Towards the end of the 1960s the fashion world re-named the long skirt: it became the maxi skirt and replaced the mini. Medium-heeled court shoes and a Baby Jane style with high heels were now preferred, though boots continued to be worn.

The department stores sold high-vamped pumps adorned with large buckles. Designers such as Bruno Magli and his one-time associate, Andrea Pfister, did not abandon their commitment to well-crafted, carefully designed shoes. Their customers were the women who continued to be guided by the *haute couture* houses of Paris. Also, Perugia continued to create comma-heeled evening pumps with extravagant frills of lace, sequins, and beads.

Sleek leather court shoes and sumptuous pumps were sought by wealthy women, and in Britain H&R Rayne continued to mass-produce for the quality end of the high street. His heels were not quite as thick as those on the Quant or Biba pumps, and he adorned them with delicate buckles and bows. In Paris, Vivier made a pump with one fat crystal ball as a heel.

But such elegance did not appeal to the young. They revolted not only against war and racial segregation but against many other social barriers. The hugely successful stage musical, *Hair*, was an assault on social conventions. It vented its rage on sexual censorship, restrictions on drug use, and the inhibitions of family and public life. Far from being insulated from this turmoil, the fashion world desperately sought to keep up with it in the styling of clothes and shoes—a trend which would continue into the next decade.

LEFT: The fashion writer, Linda O'Keefe, called the pump "the little black dress of shoes." Meaning, smart enough for any occasion. These examples, labeled Nicolette, are modestly embellished. On the left, a tiny chain sits aslant the vamp, while the shoe on the right has a narrow loop lying above the throat of the arch. The U.S. President's chic wife, Jackie Kennedy, made pumps part of her official wardrobe and signature look.

1970s
SYMBOLIC FOOTWEAR

The flame of confident rebellion dimmed with the opening of the new decade. Two more horrific assassinations in the United States, those of the anti-segregation leader, Dr Martin Luther King and the Attorney General, Robert Kennedy, ended the '60s, and the country was in turmoil over the Vietnam War. Young American men were fleeing their country to avoid conscription into the army, while thousands of families marched against the government. Oil prices caused a slump in the world economy, and the general atmosphere was subdued, angry even, but certainly not wild and joyful.

The West had lost its old social cohesion; the once-exuberant young, older now, did not settle into a shared, liberal world-view but divided into groups and factions, each with its own agenda. There were pacifists, socialists, capitalists, feminists, and voices demanding multiculturalism. All were noisy in demanding that their view prevail. The fashion scene reflected the new mood; there was no leader of fashion, no universal rule, and there were no overwhelming trends. Women dressed to identify their ideology and personality, rather than their status.

RIGHT: Many people were shocked by the appearance of Punk women because they made themselves deliberately ugly, proudly against everything that feminity represented: modesty, prettiness, and frailty. The Doc Martens boots, so masculine and so unflattering to a woman's leg were as shocking as their wild haircuts. But the Punks wanted to change traditional perceptions of women's role in society.

RIGHT: Doc Martens boots have eight eyelets, a saddle-stitched welt, and thick soles. Over the years, this defiant footwear for rebels has evolved to become mainstream everyday wear, and has spawned many imitators.

One ideology was impossible to ignore because it had a strong exhibitionist streak in demonstrating its rejection of bourgeois values. Roaming around London, female Punks sported pink and orange tufts of hair on otherwise shaven heads, tore deliberate holes in their dark stockings and marched around with their feet encased in Doc Martens workman's boots. The patent for this footwear, designed in 1940s Germany, was sold in the 1960s to the British company, R. Griggs who gave the boot distinctive yellow stitching, but retained its cushioned rubber sole, patented as AirWair.

Initially, working class boys wore these boots but by the early '70s they were the uniform of Punk boys and girls, and were rapidly adopted by copycat groups around the world. R. Griggs manufactured, also, AirWair oxfords and these maintained a steady market among women seeking comfortable footwear.

ABOVE: Mannish shoes were not new. When women began to live physically active lives, manufacturers refined men's oxfords and brogues for walking and sport. By the '70s, the brogue had become tailored, high-heeled footwear, suitable for office wear. And it was perfectly matched to the flared trousers that were fashionable.

And another, smaller tribe appeared on the streets. The feminist movement spawned a faction that furiously rejected men and traditional female roles. They wore shoes and clothes of manly style, and their hair was fiercely cropped. But they were to have an influence on fashion.

RIGHT: Entertainers favored absurdly high platforms, and this made the design trendy among the young. This inexpensive textile version sold on the high street to dedicated followers of fashion.

176

The hippie movement of the '60s suffered through its association with Charles Manson and his commune of followers who had gone on an infamous murder spree in California. Drugs and anti-social behavior stained the image of back-to-earth communes. Yet their philosophy of peace and gentle living in a "global village" was not forgotten, and their embrace of non-industrial cultures continued to inspire people.

Long boots assumed an "ethnic" look—embroidered and painted. Cowboy boots, well known for their decoration, set the standard. The Texan designer, Dave Little, is a master craftsman of cowboy boots, but his bespoke footwear is beyond the reach of most people. Biba put machine-embroidered folk designs on knee-high boots and Yves St Laurent produced a beautiful black and gold boot, his decoration referencing Russian artistic traditions.

LEFT: This boot was aimed at a market that preferred handicrafts and traditional art to mass production. Of course, this footwear was made in a factory, but shoppers were happy the embroidery imitated hand sewing and the front-laced style harked back to a nostalgic Edwardian era.

Terry
de Havilland

This English shoe designer was born Terry Higgins but changed his name in the hope of becoming an actor. He was trained as a cordwainer by his father and learnt his craft making winklepickers for Mods. After unearthing a pattern from his father's archives, de Havilland made some patchwork crocodile skin platforms to sell in a local market. His business in London took off, and in 1972 he opened Cobblers to the World, a shop which soon counted many rock stars and disco clubbers among its customers.

De Havilland also designed shoes for the movie *The Rocky Horror Show*. He re-introduced stiletto heels, but in 1979 his shop closed and his next business, Kamikaze Shoes, also failed. He was later commissioned by the clothes designers, Alexander McQueen and Anna Sui, but it was as a designer of fetish and bondage boots that he at last attained financial stability.

RIGHT: Terry de Havilland studied patterns used by his father in the 1940s, and this shoe shows the influences of his research. He has used mock croc, a material common to that period, to trim the vamp, line the platform, and cover the heel. The color, however, is definitely contemporary 1970s.

RIGHT: The designer made this glamorous mule in the '60s when he started work as a cordwainer. Low heels were anathema to Terry, so he welcomed the Spring-O-Later device introduced by the U.S. designer, Beth Levine, because it allowed him to put a stiletto heel on his mule. The vamp is probably patterned pony skin and not real leopard.

RIGHT: Older women viewed platforms as wartime fashion, but young women loved the height and comfort such shoes gave them. This design may have recalled the 1940s, but the color and chunky shape were completely up-to-date.

Other manufacturers used printed brocade on high-laced boots. This was an acknowledgment of the "flower power" mood of the hippies and peace movement. The term was applied to the pacifism of these groups, epitomized by the flower a young American woman pushed into the open end of a rifle barrel carried by a National Guard soldier.

But rock musicians moved beyond the organic protest style into something flamboyant and absolutely outrageous. David Bowie, the "King of Glam Rock," appeared in frills, make-up, and glittering sequined platform shoes. Dave Hill of the pop group Slade reveled in his outrageous high heels. Disco dancers grabbed the style with gusto: platform shoes brought height but the platform lessened the incline between heel and toe. This made platforms the perfect high heel shoes for twisting to rock music.

RIGHT: Rock music moved from protest songs with a political message to individualistic shock entertainment. Unwittingly, the rebel musicians encouraged eccentricity in artistes, such as Dave Hill and Noddy Holder of Slade, who wore eye-catching costumes and absurdly high platforms to attract attention.

RIGHT: Shiny plastic boots with low heels were aimed at energetic young dolly birds but this boot, with its curved shank and very high heel, was aimed at young women who wanted to present a more worldly image.

Terry de Havilland can be held responsible: his platform snakeskin shoes, copied from a design left by his father, sold out within days and thereafter, Terry de Havilland from his shop Cobblers to the World, was designing for flamboyant rock stars such as Bette Midler, Bowie, and Cher.

Platform boots appeared with very high heels, and on many platform shoes glossy PVC covers were used to bring wow-power to the feet. This shiny synthetic fabric came in many colors and was widely used in footwear. Oxfords came as platforms, but not in the dull style of the '40s. Now, they appeared in gleaming multi-colored covers of yellow, green, red, and blue—or they were sequined all over!

ABOVE: The mule has never fallen out of favor but, stimulated by the popularity of clog sandals such as Birkenstocks, it became modish again in the '70s. More attractive to look at, although not as effective for foot health, this high cork wedgie style was often preferred—even by women with a "hippy" lifestyle.

Some '70s platforms copied historic versions with cork or wood soles, and often had a peep toe and a sling-back strap on the heel, with a wildly patterned cover. The hysteria over this "glam rock" style led to ridiculously high platforms, although these tended to be on the feet of entertainers rather than those of women dashing to work or the disco club.

RIGHT: A high-heeled sandal uses pale blue textile, tastefully trimmed with white for a summery look. It satisfied those who thought "natural" materials nicer, or more virtuous, than synthetics.

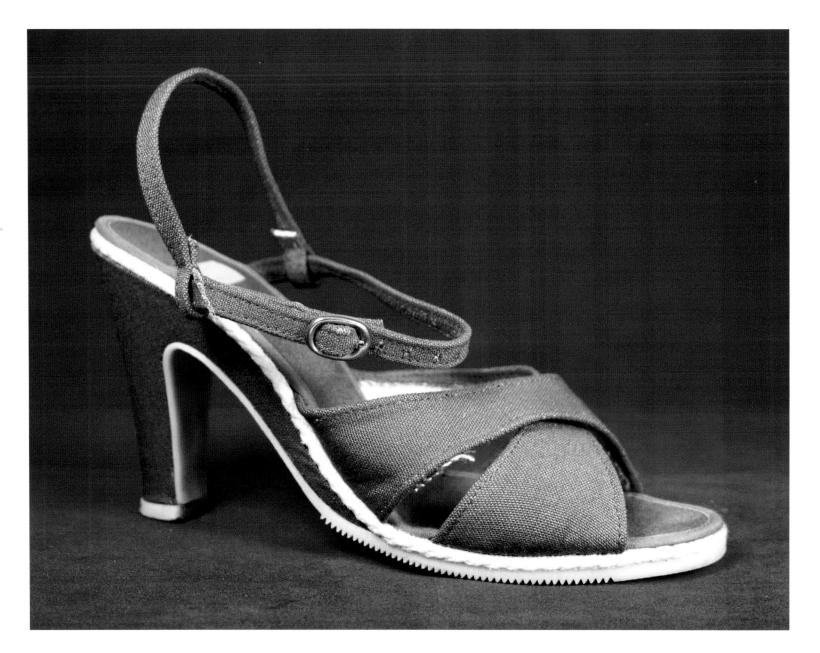

Espadrilles came in wedgie platforms and proved very popular—canvas, cork, and string being authentic earth materials. And wedgie clogs were revived, many with platform toes, with natural dark leather covers. Armando Pollini made a clog with a plastic bottom unit and leather upper. Called "Candies" in the U.S., they sold, with various modifications, to both men and women. In their wake, came—inevitably—the mule. This time, it looked like a relative of the old-time clog, with a deep, practical cover of leather but with a high, sturdy heel. They were also given canvas or patchwork suede covers. People liked clogs and mules, because they looked good whether worn with socks, stockings, or bare feet.

As ever, there was an unchanging market for frothy, frivolous shoes but it was a hidden retail area, becoming visible only towards the end of the decade. Snakeskin enjoyed a revival, preferably dyed in interesting colors. The American, Herbert Levine, made a sling-back of transparent vinyl dotted with spots of colored snakeskin. Pink croc skin was used for mules, and H&R Rayne made green high-heeled sandals with an ankle strap; and Bruno Mugli designed an apple green court shoe of great elegance.

BELOW: The high vamp and chunky heel remained fashionable with the young, who were also delighted by the glossy plastic cover and the glaring color combinations offered by contemporary shoes. The boxy shape was worn with short skirts or flared trousers.

LEFT: Rosetti have a strong historical sense, and this high-heeled sandal has an unexpected source of reference. Once a leisure shoe, the spectator, or correspondent, is reborn with cut-outs and brogue punching, to emerge as a classy mule.

ABOVE: This court shoe with its daring extension of the vamp and the counter creates a geometric abstract. Seeing this, it is easy to understand why Paloma Picasso, daughter of the artist, is one of Rossetti's clients.

Rosetti
Fratelli

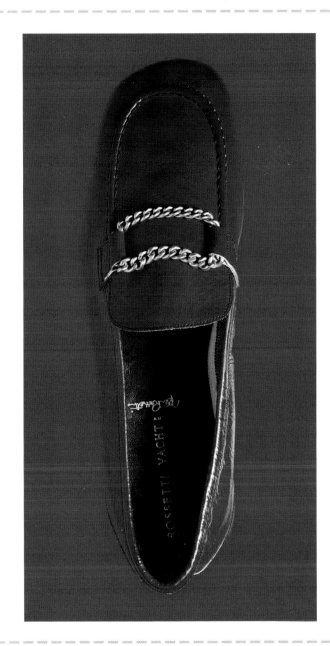

BELOW: The snug ankle boot was first seen in the '50s, but Rossetti re-creates it with elegance. The suede cover is draped from the ankle to fold over the vamp, and the heel is of the same material as the cover. It is altogether beautifully crafted.

This high-end Italian manufacturer was opened in 1955 by two Milanese brothers, Renzo and Renato Rosetti. They began by making men's shoes, but quickly caught on to the vogue for "unisex" styles in the 1970s. They found a ready market for crafted women's versions of gentlemen's footwear and were especially successful in the USA.

Renzo's three sons later took over the business and went on to develop a global brand of sophisticated, classic styling. The company's shoe production continues to rely on craftsmanship and its marketing emphasizes individual attention to each shoe. Rosetti Fratelli footwear is made for the elite market in the U.S., Europe, and China, and clients include Paloma Picasso and Lauren Bacall.

LEFT: Mannish shoes suited the feminist mood and the wide pants of the decade—so Rossetti responded with his Yacht range. The casually looped chain, in place of a stern buckle, diminishes the impression of masculinity.

The '70s was dogged by a pervasive interest in "health" shoes. A Danish designer and yoga enthusiast, Anne Kalso, made Earth shoes in which the heel sat lower than the toe. She claimed this was a natural pose for the foot. They were copied by a Canadian manufacturer, Roots, but, after the initial excitement, these negative heels proved unpopular. Birkenstock sandals, and clogs were considered much better health choices.

Loafers found regular sales, especially after JP Tod introduced his Gommino, a soft moccasin with rubber-studded soles. The Italian, Rosetti Fratelli, produced loafers with canvas lining that allowed the wearer to abandon their socks and he exported a range of mannish shoes for women to the U.S. where his footwear was well received.

BELOW: Low heels were fashionable, but this shoe made concession to those women who saw footwear as an accessory to enhance the foot. There was always a market for the pretty and elegant, such as this shoe with a graceful slope to its heel, a soft suede cover, and its decorative two-tone bow.

All these utility shoes were ideal for women going on protest marches. American women were not interested in looking feminine while they were demonstrating against the Vietnam War and certainly did not want to be uncomfortable as they marched. They dressed in denim jeans or overalls and rugged shoes made for walking, or even the occasional kicking action. Overseas women in Britain and Europe took their cue from their sisters across the Atlantic.

Not all women were on the march in political protest, and in the high street shops, fashion kept an ethnic look that reflected a gentle multicultural world-view. Women's clothes took a romantic turn, with long, flared skirts, and full gathered sleeves. Pants were wide legged bell-bottoms, while disco evening-wear was spangled and sequined.

LEFT: Leisure footwear became increasingly important. When Diego Della Valle took samples of his Italian family's crafted footwear to New York, the family's '70s range, Gommino—a moccasin with a pebbled sole—was marketed as a driving shoe. Comfortable and elegant, it remains bestseller casual wear for men and women. Della Valle called his U.S. company JP Tod, and it is well known now as a manufacturer of quality footwear.

LEFT: The satin cover implies this sandal was intended for eveningwear. Bare toes, and cutaways that leave the arch exposed, give them sex appeal. Although the open cut may have looked better teamed with a narrow heel, the sandal has been given a fashionably chunky heel.

BELOW: This pump heralds a change in popular taste. Its heel is high and has a triangular form, and the subtle color also made this suede shoe distinctive from bright contemporary fashion. A little flower cut-out on the vamp adds modest decoration.

But designers picked up on the jeans and dungarees workman look, and shoppers could buy mannish blazers, shirts, knitted waistcoats, and loose pleated pants. High-heeled spectators and oxfords suited this latter look, as did brogues, but the trailing skirts were matched with suede shoes in soft colors, with ankle straps or cross bars.

There was a hint of '30s footwear design from the *haut couture* houses. This was not a time for high fashion bravado although the quality house, Charles Jourdan maintained steady sales. Norman Parkinson photographed the Texan model, Jerry Hall, in ankle strap high heels, and even showed her barefoot in simple, earthy style. The Somali beauty, Iman, was draped in cheesecloth, an organic fabric favored by the hippies but in a gown that reflected her ethnic origins. She wore low-heeled cream shoes with a woven leather cover.

Parkinson also photographed an Italian model at the races wearing narrow pants, a straight three-quarter coat, a spotted cravat, and a trilby hat. High heeled ankle boots adorned her feet, and the picture was captioned "unisex fashion," a hot slogan during this time of active feminist protest.

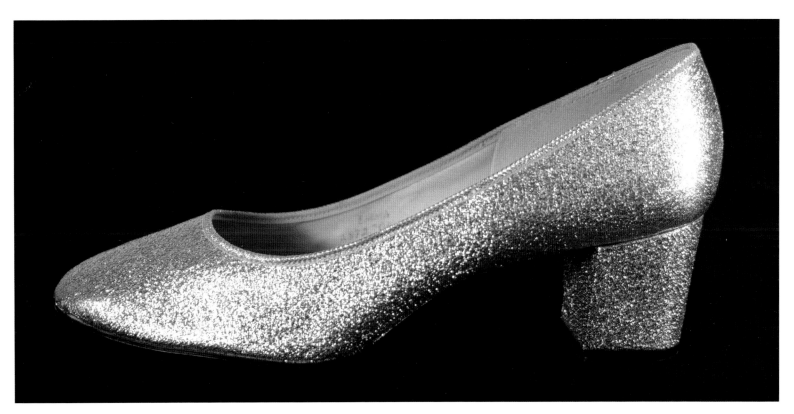

LEFT: A very plain pump with a trendy squat heel relies, for its beauty, on the shimmering silver textile used on the cover.

ABOVE: A textile loop assures the buyer that the inner sole is bouncing, meaning it is soft, springy, and very comfortable even if worn over long periods.

LEFT: As they became regular high street fashion, Doc Martens came out in a daring range of colors—red, green, and yellow—and many products were aimed specifically at women, but all retained the stitched welt, thick sole, and AirWair comfort inner soles.

R. Griggs

Based in Northampton, England, this family business opened in 1901. Its aims were very specific: the manufacture of workingmen's boots. To this end, in 1959 it acquired the licence for a boot with a cushioned rubber sole from the German manufacturer Dr Maertens. Calling the footwear Doc Martens, R. Griggs initially sold to policemen and mail workers. The company gave the eight-eyelet boot a PVC cover and yellow stitching, but was surprised when British teenagers adopted it as part of their "uniform."

The brutal appearance of Doc Martens appealed to young rebels but gradually became acceptable at all social levels. Sales rocketed worldwide, and the product had many color and style variations. Even the Vatican placed orders for the boots and the patented sole, AirWair, was used by the designer Manolo Blahnik. In the 1990s R. Griggs became involved in litigation to protect its design against copies. Suffering financial losses during that decade, the company moved its operations to China.

BELOW: In the '40s, Dr Maertens sold walking shoes to German women, and when R. Griggs bought the name, they maintained the tradition of sturdy, well-designed footwear. This chunky T-bar has brogue decoration, thick weatherproof soles, and a heel loop to pull the shoe onto the foot. This is designed as a woman's shoe but similar sandal styles are made for men.

Vogue magazine was driven (out of courtesy, perhaps) to ask if bad taste is a bad thing. Hot pants and fishnet tights, peasant skirts, denim dungarees, and disconnected patterns jumbled together—all were acceptable in this confused decade when every woman wanted to make her own fashion statement. Footwear too veered from ugly sandals to brogues, to gorgeous strappy platforms in shimmering tones.

The political atmosphere was in much the same state as fashion. Aggressive pressure groups were strident in claiming their corner; the Vietnam War was over but now was replaced by fears that the Cold War between the USSR (Soviet Russia) and the West would escalate into military action, while the constant strike actions of labor unions in Britain caused despair, anger, and sheer weariness.

LEFT: Black patent leather is, by its very nature, sleek and sophisticated and its oily gleam suits eveningwear. This pump has a grown-up heel and the round toe has a frilled vamp.

LEFT: As the decade drew to a close, heels grew higher. They remained sturdy, as did the long and mannish vamp, the kind of shape that was best worn with wide pants. The green cover, too, reflected the '70s love of shoes in hard, bright color. The gold metal trims bring a superior touch of authority.

LEFT: Fashion was beginning to emerge from the chaotic decades of rebellion, health shoes, and little girl heels. This slender sandal, on a demanding high heel, has narrow bands cut with a tiny zigzag edge. This sandal is a bold statement against health footwear, and a brisk retort to anti-feminine feminism.

BELOW: Foot health remained a hot issue, so this high heel was sold as good for feet, and not for its sex appeal. This sassy mule is stamped Homy Ped of Germany, from their range, Fussform, made from "natural wood" and "genuine leather" and has a contoured insole. The reassured buyer felt good as well as gorgeous.

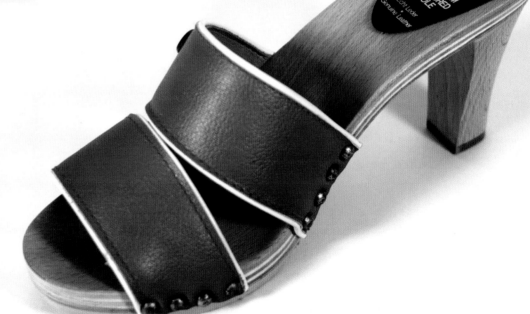

Footwear had ceased to be a fashion statement. Shoes were no longer a simple symbol of wealth and status. As the decade progressed choice of footwear made a clear announcement: Birkenstocks spoke of ecological concerns, and canvas espadrilles revealed a personal life of caring vegetarianism and pacifism. Embroidered boots pronounced an all-embracing cultural view, while court shoes indicated a quiet conservatism, and Doc Martens gave a worrying hint of youthful rebellion. Footwear revealed, in the 1970s, the wearer's moral stance.

Women began to feel growing impatience towards the social unrest and grew tired of a free-for-all fashion scene that lacked discipline, direction, or artistry. Much of it was unattractive and ill groomed, even if this expressed a high-minded feminism that derided the tradition of women dressing well and using cosmetics—that sort of behavior was viewed as an affront to gender equality. Well, the majority were no longer convinced.

The relaxed, but well made look of the American clothes worn in movies by Diane Keeton in *Annie Hall*, or Faye Dunaway in *Network* looked good after the muddle of the previous few years. A clean, cared-for appearance in a fit, healthy body seemed preferable to the careless bohemian or the plain, earnest look of the social worker. The time was ripe for gorgeous sandals, pretty pumps, and chic court shoes, for high heels, polish, and grooming.

BELOW: Roland Cartier responded to the growing demand for sophistication from women who longed for alluring, beautiful shoes. His vamp has a wavy edge and he has veiled the toes with lace. The high heel is of the new triangular shape and his silver is leather, not a glittering, or sequined textile. His design offered an alternative to the girly, the mannish, and the chunky heel.

RIGHT: Dolly Parton, singer and musician, defied all idealist talk of a gender-free, uni-sex world. With blonde locks and deep bosom, she displayed shoulders of exaggerated width, showed lots of leg, and put her bare feet into transparent high heels. The look epitomized the power dressing of independent career women.

1980s
POWER STYLE

Feminism developed unexpected spin-offs that became apparent in the '80s. Instead of a gender equality that dissolved the differences between the sexes, women emerged as sexually proud and confident. They did not choose to be like men, but neither did they reject the opposite sex—the only choices the '70s activists seemed to offer. '80s woman found strength in being female, and reveled in clear gender differences.

In the U.S. the singer, Cher, appeared on one record cover as a scantily clad Viking and Dolly Parton aped the old blonde glamour of a Hollywood '50s movie star. Both women are extremely talented musicians, singers, and businesswoman, but they believed they were empowered by their physical attributes. Margaret Thatcher became the first woman Prime Minister of Great Britain, and she represented another face of female emancipation. She was ambitious in a man's world, fearless and dressed in impeccably tailored clothes. She did not pretend indifference to her appearance, nor did she adopt a mannish style.

Women began to dress for their careers and not for political protest. Career-minded women who took their cue from Mrs Thatcher assumed a power-dressing mode. They donned suits with fitted jackets and wide shoulders over narrow skirts, and were shod in impressive footwear. To flaunt their wealth and success, they chose shoes by Manolo Blahnik. His high inverted pyramid heels and long toes, the instep decorated with thin straps, denoted distinction, money, and style.

LEFT: Sandals moved from sensible to elegant. This has a very narrow vamp, cut in a curve to emphasize brightly painted toes, with a thin strap at the ankle exposing a bare heel. Its appearance and intent were far from those of foot molding clog sandals.

BELOW: This handsome shoe with its dignified silhouette and high heel was a style much sought after by an emerging group of assertive women who dressed for success.

H&R Rayne produced patchwork leather and Andre Pfister made some of the most beautiful shoes, his covers brocaded or cleverly strapped. Charles Jourdan favored high arches on his stilettos, while Paul Mayer created decorative heels. The cover was demure, but as the woman walked away her heels flashed gems or carved flowers. The French describe these as *venez-y-voir* or "come hither" shoes. Farragamo gave dignified dark leather very high, very thin, stilettos. The sound of heels clicking down the office corridor was the new sound of female power.

Stiletto heels were a vital element in the images presented by rock stars and politicians alike. Cher may have posed naked, but her stage appearances were in gorgeous theatrical costume and her shoes were as erotic as her voice. High heels, disco dancing glitz, and daring were her style. Ms. Parton relished her appearance, showy, and big chested, as she sashayed about in tight gowns complimented with shiny red heels or stitched and appliquéd high cowboy boots.

ABOVE: Patchwork, reminiscent of hippy bags of the '60s, returned but this '80s version is a restrained modification of neat triangles in gold and silver leather.

LEFT: In the '80s, touches of gold and silver were perceived as radiating hints of wealth and success. This court shoe was designed as a shoe to impress but not overwhelm the onlooker. (It has an extra hidden symbol of success with its inner sole of silver leather.)

Boots remained standard footwear but now, they were high heeled and decorated in wild fashion patterns without obvious reference to gypsy or ethnic folk art. Cowboy decoration was increasingly popular although the designs became ornate and colorful in a way unknown on the cattle ranch. Other boots carried colorful decorations of stripes, checks, and metal studs, or they were piped with gold. Short ankle boots were folded and buckled around the ankle, or trimmed with fur.

The young were stomping round in colored Doc Martens, casually matched with soft floral dresses or mini skirts. They chose boots with bizarre and dazzling decorations—a sequined Union Jack pattern was favored by Punks. The famous Biba shop had closed down, proving the market for the boho, hippy look had declined drastically. Specialist shoe shops appeared on the high street. China was beginning to manufacture footwear and their products were trickling into the West. The boots and shoes copied western trends, but they were plastic and cheap.

RIGHT: A high heel and exuberant color give this sandal a carefree mood but it is not made for carefree dressing. It is elegant and chic, and comes from Yves St Laurent.

BELOW: This is no ordinary wedgie. Charles Jourdan has given the wedge a sculptured, curved surface and then, for his straps, he uses plaited leather, not the raffia so often seen on similar styles. The T-strap and sugar pink color add to the distinctive quality of this sandal.

Charles
Jourdan

The firm of Charles Jourdan opened in Paris in 1919. In the 1930s it was the first manufacturer to use advertisements to sell shoes. Twenty years later, Charles Jourdan shoes were being sold in Britain and the company was licensed to Christian Dior. The company developed as a high-end ready-to-wear manufacturer, with a strong reputation for the innovative use of new fabrics and interesting design.

Charles Jourdan expanded to the USA where its shoes were distributed by the giant retailer Genesco. When the dictator of the Philippines, Ferdinand Marcos, was toppled in 1986, his wife Imelda won notoriety for her vast collection of shoes, many of which were enviable Charles Jourdan numbers. The company was sold to Genesco, and the last family member involved, Roland Jourdan, retired in 1981. Lux Diversity bought the company in 2002, and since 2005 Josephus Thimister has been chief designer.

ABOVE: Charles Jourdan proves he can do exuberant and glitzy. On this sandal, he tied the straps into a bow, and made them glitter with tiny colored crystals. But it is the heel that gets the attention. A metal rod is held onto the sole but it bulges into a little ball on the heel tip. The silver of this metal is echoed in the silver of the beaded straps and the inner sole.

LEFT: This delicious pink sling-back is from Charles Jourdan, one of the great masters of shoe design. The gilt decoration makes a small concession to the glittery decoration often preferred during this decade.

The U.S. clothing company, Gap, persuaded young shoppers to wear well-made jeans, neat shirts, and sweaters and this chic casual look replaced the slovenly protest appearance of old. Oxfords, pumps, and loafers fitted this style. There was also a market for low-heeled pumps among women who admired the romantic soft fashion of Diana, Princess of Wales. She was a tall girl married to a short man, so she avoided very high heels.

LEFT: The silhouette reveals its historic inspiration—the round toe and high heel recalling the '40s, a time of efficient women and top secret backroom war operations. This busy reference pleased the '70s working woman.

The high-end designers made darling little pumps, wrapped with big bows or adorned with large buckles. The Punk liking for studs and metalwork decoration crept into mainstream style, and low-heeled shoes showed hints of Punk. Even Yves St Laurent studded the ankle strap on a high-heeled sandal. Embroidered Oriental slippers were given thin rubber soles; Chinese fabric peasant shoes, round-toed, and very flat, with a buttoned cross-bar made comfortable Baby Jane-style shoes.

The baby boomers were close to middle age; they needed to look after their feet, and they needed exercise to maintain their figure. Everyone began to jog and keep fit, while gyms and health clubs sprang up on every corner. The movie star, Jane Fonda, marketed numerous videos teaching vigorous aerobic workouts. It was no longer fashionable to dismiss sport as a dreary discipline. Indeed, sport was evolving into high entertainment, and professional players attracted huge fan bases. Martina Navratilova was at the start of her spectacular tennis career, and along with her fellow player, Chrissie Evert, had become a sporting icon.

LEFT: Cowboy boots have an inward sloping heel and are often lavishly decorated. This fashion version is a good copy of the style, and uses the tooled leather method traditionally employed to mark cowboy boots. Fashionable young women loved these masculine but decorative boots, pairing them with jeans or drifting skirts.

ABOVE: Dull gold became an everyday color for accessories, such as bags and shoes. These pumps, given a thick X on the vamp, made reliable office wear. Round-toed and low-heeled, they were comfortable but smart.

LEFT: A cheeky English designer, showing an unconventional, daring spirit, decorated high platform boots with a brash and glittering Union Jack. Showcased by the Spice Girls pop group, they were also snatched up by Punks and subsequently could be found on main street.

Women were confident there were few gender barriers to inhibit their aspirations and ambitions. More and more women invaded areas traditionally reserved for men. The first woman to sail single-handed on a non-stop circumnavigation of the world was Kay Cottee in 1988. In 1975, a Japanese woman, Junke Tabei climbed Mount Everest and was followed by Stacey Allinson in 1988. Women demanded the right gear for their new sporting adventures.

The manufacturers responded. Blue Ribbon Sports was a distributor of sports shoes until, in the early '70s, a founder of the company, Bill Bowerman invented the Waffle Trainer with a lightweight grid-like sole. The tennis champion, Jimmy Connors, wore them when he won Wimbledon in 1978. The company became Nike and their carefully designed shoes became big footwear items in the 1980s.

Both Nike and another sports footwear manufacturer, Adidas, made shoes that paid attention to ergonomics, foot shape, and muscle movement. But, as more and more women began to buy the rubber-soled footwear, so little feminine notes, touches of pink or purple, were added to the shoes. City women traveled to work in their trainers then changed into their stiletto heels in the office. This habit started in New York when the public transport employees went on strike and people were obliged to walk or cycle to get to work. But more and more trainers were seen on the feet of shoppers or those wandering around leisure centers.

The scientific thinking behind trainers convinced shoppers: they appreciated the attention to the structure of the foot, its need to "breathe," and the accommodation of toe spread and movement. Also, these sports shoes were made in lightweight fabric, much lighter and easier to wear than leather walking shoes.

This overwhelming concern with health and comfort was, perhaps, not an unexpected development in women's footwear but, fortunately, it did not deter the makers of delicious shoes designed to ornament the feet. Sensing the rich pickings of a global market combined with the threat of competitive manufacturers in the Far East, the established companies and designers began to concentrate on the production of beautiful shoes.

BELOW: Manufacturers sensed that the conventional divide between day and evening-wear was closing. They began to make shoes like this one that could serve for all events. The rich purple and patterned satin of the cover has a formal appearance, but the low wedge gives it an easy, comfortable look.

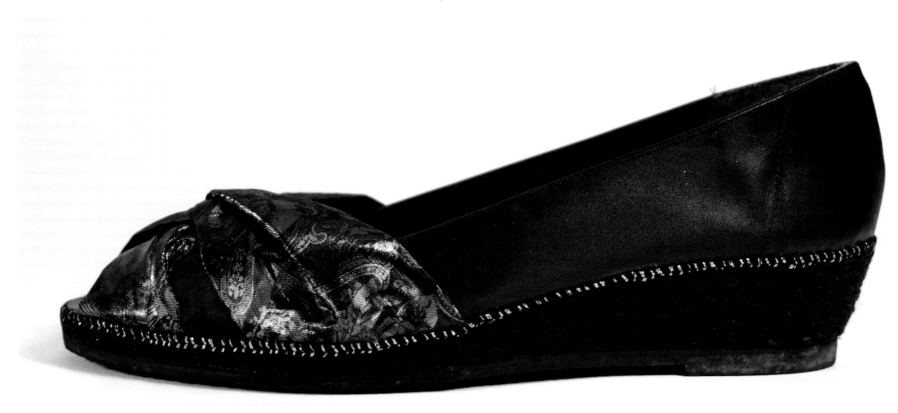

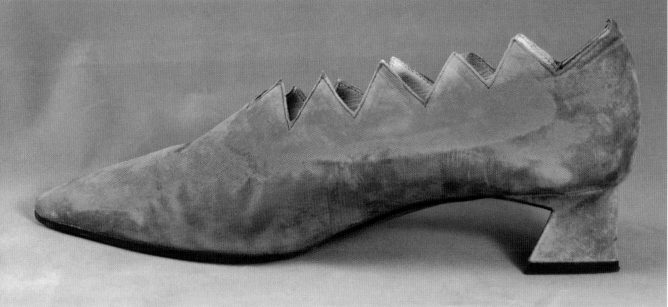

BELOW: The Baby Jane made a comeback, but looking curiously mature. The stacked heel and the broad crossbar cancel the little girl look and make the style into something for grownups to wear. They came from the English manufacturer Ravel.

ABOVE: Designers were beginning to explore the potential brought by computer technology. The English manufacturer, Pied-a-Terre, made this quirky shoe with its jagged throat, repeated in the angular cut of the heel. Women who wanted to express their individuality were pleased to have access to distinctive and unusual designs such as this one.

Fashion writers were persuaded to focus on footwear, and remind their readers that beautiful shoes were sexy and stylish. Shoes became a barometer of changing fashion, and as such, styles dated really quickly—so fashionable footwear needed to be frequently replaced. Companies began to fight for recognition as the makers of classy, enviable shoes, believing this was the best argument against the cheap imports.

BELOW: This shoe is, at heart, a classic pump, but a small cutaway on the counter makes it a sling-back. Andre Pfister created this smart compromise between an open shoe and dignified closed footwear.

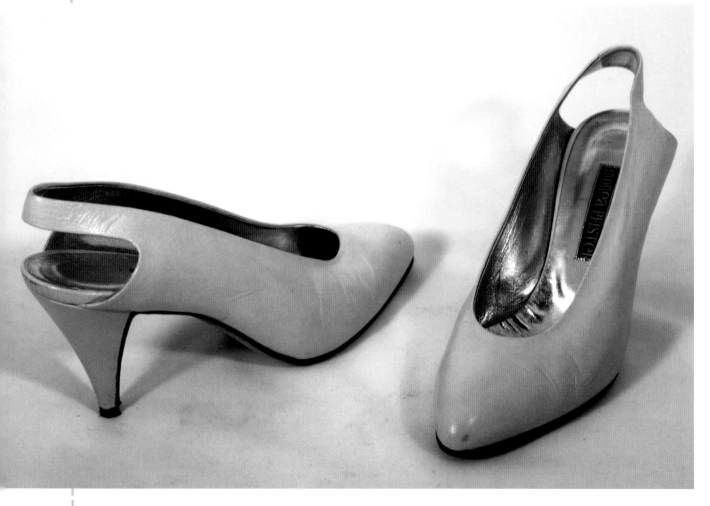

ABOVE: This shoe is not blatantly eye-catching, however, it would delight most women. It has a flattering design, enfolding the foot in a waved throat that wraps in a semi-circle over the arch. The soft tone of the suede is a perfect foil for the pearl drop buttons.

Andrea
Pfister

A ndrea Pfister was educated in Italy and Switzerland and was quickly recognized by his fellow craftsmen as an extraordinary designer. He was only twenty-three years old when he was awarded the prize for Best International Footwear Design. The fashion houses of Jean Patou and Lanvin commissioned designs from him, and in 1967 he opened his own boutique in Paris. He designed for Anne Klein and Bruno Magli and opened a second outlet in Italy. In 1987 he received the Grand Fashion Medal of Honor as Best International Footwear Designer.

Pfister creates for fashion houses and has ready-to-wear collections. He has a studio in Positano, Italy, where he creates his luxurious shoes with ornaments of sequins, embroidery, and textured leather. His footwear is reproduced under licence to manufacturers in Japan, Turkey, Spain, and South Africa.

BELOW: The U.S. department store, Neiman Marcus, commissioned this shoe from Andre Pfister. Cleverly, he takes a classic court and gives it a bold color mix, but he adds a special detail—he cuts into the geometry of the stripes on the vamp, thus causing a delightful asymmetry. It was this kind of shoe, bold, colorful, and smart, that pleased the '80s superwoman.

LEFT: The great champion, Martina Navratilova, powers her way across the court. She is muscular and athletic, and is wearing Nike footwear, designed to ease the foot and improve speed.

Designers began to emerge as an important element in this changing footwear market. Names such as Charles Jourdan, Manola Blahnik, Philippe Model, and Stuart Weitzman began to seep into the public conscious. This strategy gave impetus to young art and fashion students who were able to contemplate a serious and well paid career in footwear manufacture. The old, established Cordwainer College in London, England, developed an excellent course of craftsmanship and study for these students. But the women's footwear industry did not foresee that the products of sports shoe manufacturers would be on the shopping list of every high fashionista.

ABOVE: The wide pebbled sole turns up at the toes, where the rubber pebbles ensure the foot's grip will hold firm, even if the wearer lurches or stumbles. It is multicolored and embellished with stripes but this does not detract from its ergonomic structure and athletic purpose.

RIGHT: This sportswear has a protective padded cover and firmly grips the ankle. The sole slopes inward from the toes, a design detail that helped ease movement. The red was chosen, initially, to please women buyers although men were becoming less conventional in the color of their footwear.

RIGHT: This shoe is uncompromising: it expresses no-nonsense power while using feminine tones of gold and green. The high straight heel and long vamp balanced wide shouldered jackets, flared pants, or short, straight skirts. They did not suit soft, flowing garments.

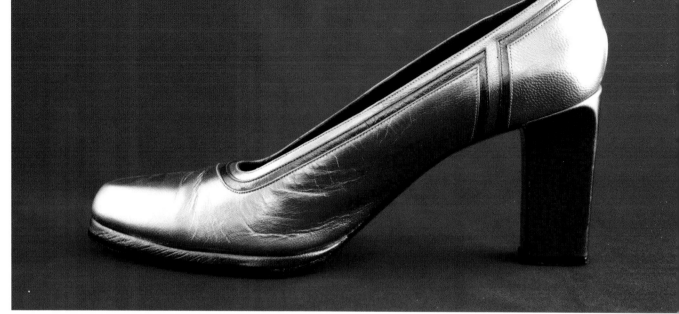

In the '80s, widespread affluence in the West allowed people to afford changing fashions as well as travel all over the world. Women wanted pretty, easy shoes to wear in warm holiday climates, on the beach, or strolling round picturesque harbors. Excellent and imaginative designs were applied to sandals. The Kork-Ease with a cork wedge sole and buffalo leather crisscross vamp had sold in the '70s and continued to be popular in the '80s. Now it came in colored leather, flashy silver, and gold glitter.

LEFT: A summer shoe, more formal than a sandal, has a peep-toe and inward curve to the low heel. It is cute, relaxed and intended for leisurewear rather than dress for the office. The designer, Franco Caresana, made it.

KORK-EASE
The Original ®
SINCE 1953

LEFT: The Kork-Ease was initially manufactured in small quantities from small premises in New York, but demand soon increased output. The chief salesman claimed the sandal was so comfortable it could be worn to bed. Made from organic cork and leather, the Kork-Ease and its variations, has remained popular since its first appearance.

LEFT: Champion tennis player, Serena Williams, hosted the unveiling of the Nike 2008 Women's Fall Line in California. Her presence confirmed that manufacturers were treating sportswomen with the attention they deserved.

ABOVE: This is from the Nike Shox range and it is made for women. It is designed emphatically for athletic wear, but the lightness of this footwear, combined with the color mix of pink and silver, caused many to purchase the shoe for leisure wear and rambling.

Nike

LEFT: A molded sole has the heel raised on four shock absorbent pillars, adding to the comfort and stability of the shoe.

BELOW: Nike was never afraid of color, and knew their female customers would appreciate the mood of fun this brought to their trainers. This style is part of the range called Nike Air Huarache Racer.

The American businessmen Phil Knight and Bill Bowerman opened a sports shoe company in 1962, later calling it Nike after the Greek goddess of victory. Nike distributed the Japanese brand Tiger until Bowerman invented a lightweight grid-soled sports shoe in 1974. He made the prototype by toasting a polyurethane sole in a waffle iron! The Waffle trainer was an international bestseller, and thereafter Nike led a major manufacturing trend towards footwear dedicated to health, comfort, and ease of movement.

Nike was a leader in athletic and exercise shoes, devoting research to improved material and design. For example, it developed the Air-Sole cushioning system for basketball footwear, the Air Jordan. During the 1980s Nike moved into mainstream footwear. In 2002 the company acquired the much-loved U.S. sports footwear company, Converse, but maintained its identity as a separate brand.

BELOW: This crazy, curved wedgie, dazzling in its stripes, is not the creation of a master designer, but comes from Next, a major retailer on the high streets of Britain. But history has told us that it has long been the fate of the jobbing cordwainer to remain anonymous, which seems a pity.

ABOVE: Injection molding, a technological advance, made plastic shoes in one piece at very little cost. These Jelly shoes came in the cheerful colors that the material allowed, and were intended for casual or beachwear but, despite this, there were women who demanded a heel. This version was made for them.

BELOW: Plastic sandals gained a certain vogue and came in many guises. This style, with its perforated straps and sole, aimed to prevent the fabric from becoming hot and sticky, a problem then found frequently in plastic, and were intended as utterly informal garden or beach wear. Let's hope it stayed in those places.

Shoppers had a choice, also, of other interesting sandals—with transparent covers on cork soles, plastic flowers as decoration, two-tone twisted straps, or striped wedges in PVC. And there were "comfort" designs with rubber soles, sturdy crossbars, and cut-out covers. But the most copied design came from Andre Pfister. He created the Deauville in 1979, this pretty, open basket weave plastic sandal really took off during the '80s. The design was a combination of shoe and sandal, so it had a formal air that reassured its wearers. This was a sandal that could easily move from the beach, to the stores, and on to an informal holiday meal.

RIGHT: Baby Boomer hero, Tina Turner, had no qualms about age when she donned a tiny dress and high heels. Her energy as she danced and sang was reassuring. Everyone in the audience was convinced health and fashion could ward off the effects of ageing.

1990s
GLAMOUR AND STATUS

The 1990s was a decade of great affluence, and women were not afraid to spend. Battles for equality or the pleas of environmentalists were now hazy memories, blotted out by the fun of freedom and money. The glitter of power dressing blossomed into an extravaganza of lavish fashion. In tandem, shoes also assumed an important role as signals of glamour, financial freedom, and strong female sexuality.

The urge to dress like men had metamorphosed into an acceptance that women could wear both boots and pants and that they could move and act with indifference to "special" female manners. No one blinked an eye when *Vogue* photographed Lisa Marie Presley dressed up in faux GI army clothes in imitation of her famous father. The singer k d Lang had no qualms dressing in a manly way and neither was her audience much bothered.

Political concerns were overcome by more personal fears for ill-health and old age. The pop singer Tina Turner, Queen of Rock 'n' Roll, was an inspiration to aging baby boomers. Her show clothes were skimpy and glittery and her hair was wild and thick. Despite physically demanding dance routines, she strutted her stuff in vertiginous heels—and she was over fifty years old. She wore variations of the standard dance shoe, which had an ankle strap and a peep-toe.

Nineteenth century corsets came back into fashion, now constructed from strong but pliable modern fabrics. They were called bustiers, to be worn not as underwear but as outerwear. Blouses or tops shrunk to uncover the midriff, while pants sat low on the hip. These styles were an expression of the thoroughly independent modern woman.

To fit this mood, Stuart Weitzman made curved heels covered in crystals and Ferragamo produced black velvet crisscrossed straps on a thin, high heel. Other designers made twisted heels or heels shaped like chair legs, or heels of twisted metal. Technology allowed a new freedom in shaping footwear, the computer being able to calculate formerly tricky measurement and loading stress with absolute accuracy. Designers could let their imaginations run free. Technology also made the coloring and patterning of materials much easier, and the designers were given a range of constantly changing choices.

BELOW: The American designer, Stuart Weitzman is famous for his use of unusual materials and interesting designs. These terrific corded silk sandals swank through life on heels constructed from a dazzling diamante ball stuck on top of a thin straight metal rod.

ABOVE: The Swarovski crystal company, who has a long history of making sparkling glasswork and jewelery beads, started to attract fashion designers. Among the first was Versace who wreathed this heel with the glitter of crystals.

RIGHT: This sandal is a signature piece from Versace. In an unusual design twist, he has given it two wide but unconnected straps, a gold inner sole and a stiletto heel. The crystal beads are wildly colored but beautifully arranged. And this sandal has the quality Versace guarantees to deliver—sex appeal.

The Italian designer Gianni Versace relished these advances. His color combinations were wild and he made clever use of the latest synthetic stretch fabrics, such as Lycra and Spandex. His fabrics were patterned with Renaissance images in hot sharp tones. He dressed his models in plunging necklines, in skirts split to the waist, and in high, strapped shoes. Here was no concession to power dressing but instead blatant sexuality.

In the previous decade, the designer Armani had reigned supreme with his subtle tones and triangular-shaped silhouettes. But now Versace swept away old-fashioned good taste, telling women to "show your wealth, your youth, your curves and your tan." His models wore high heels with rhinestone decoration or big ornamental buckles. Then the raunchy young singer Madonna wore his bold clothes in one of his major advertising campaigns.

The baby boomers formed a wealthy market now, and women were beginning to rely on ornate clothes and elegant legs to maintain a youthful appearance. Shoe manufacturers began to emphasize the quality and elegance of their brand, while shoppers were persuaded by the constant presentation of designer logos and repetitive fashion photography to buy products from certain reliable craftsmen-designers. Meanwhile Versace promoted his super models, a carefully chosen group of young women who were constantly displayed in magazines, newspapers, and on TV. He made them celebrity figures, enviably groomed, beautiful, and daring. Women everywhere wanted to look like them, wearing Versace clothes and fantastic shoes.

BELOW: Elements of the cowboy boot—a low slanting heel, long pointed toe, and baroque patterning—have been used on this pant boot. Reptile skin covers the toe, and it is used again on the swirled decoration appliqued on the vamp.

RIGHT: The court shoe is modest, if shaped with superb elegance, and the quiet gold-trimmed folds around the heel give a mere hint of the butterfly on the heel. This mix of the classic and the unexpected was a strong design element during this decade.

ABOVE: A wonderfully shiny butterfly rests on the heel, causing surprise when the wearer walks away. The slightly curved narrow heel forms a perfect stem to support it.

Manolo
Blahnik

L ike fellow shoemaker Jimmy Choo, Manolo Blahnik became well known when his shoes were named and adored by the stars of *Sex in the City*. Of Czech and Spanish origin, Blahnik studied law in Switzerland and art in Paris. He began working with shoes in a small London shop, Zapata, which he later bought. By 1978 his shoes were being sold in Bloomingdales, the New York department store, and he opened his own New York shop a year later. His American business partner George Malkemus developed a distribution network across the States, and an outlet in Hong Kong was opened in 1991.

Blahnik has collaborated with many couture designers, such as Galliano for Chanel, Calvin Klein, Caroline Herrera, and Oscar de la Renta. He claims to be inspired by Roger Vivier, and aims to create quality shoes that have a little risqué "hooker" chic.

LEFT: The fashion model, Monica Belluci, is dressed for glamour in fitting tribute to her footwear. Blahnik has made "fringes" of drop pearls to dangle provocatively over her exposed feet, which are scarcely dressed in thin straps and a high, high heel.

LEFT: The old gold satin cover makes a beautiful setting for the large diamante buckle fringed with black, white, and gold beads. The very high thin heel flares out at the top, and the whole shoe has a sumptuous, tailored appearance.

BELOW: Kid leather has been used to make this mule with its low kitten heel. The sides of the vamp extend to the shank. On the front of the vamp is a cluster of pearls, crystals, and topaz-colored beads falling with a natural grace against the gold kid. It is Blahnik's genius to avoid a contrived appearance, no matter how complex his ornament.

Yet women continued to pursue jobs and careers, to commute AND run their homes. High heels were glamorous but difficult to wear right through the day. A Canadian born designer, Patrick Cox provided the answer with his Wannabe loafers in 1993: they had a bulky shape and an exaggerated profile carefully constructed to flatter the leg.

He made them flat and with stacked heels, and the Wannabes were an instant success. He made them with Union Jacks printed on the cover, as high-heeled crocodile skin versions, or two-tone spectators. Copies later appeared, and the Wannabe band over the tongue was given a buckle or cut as a thick triangle. Women wore them with pant suits, tweed skirts, and jeans.

Men's shoes designed for women were commonplace in the market. Robert Clergerie ensured his oxfords were supple and cut for comfort; Charles Jourdan produced a sophisticated and elegant variation of Doc Martens. At every level of society, women took to comfort in their workaday lives.

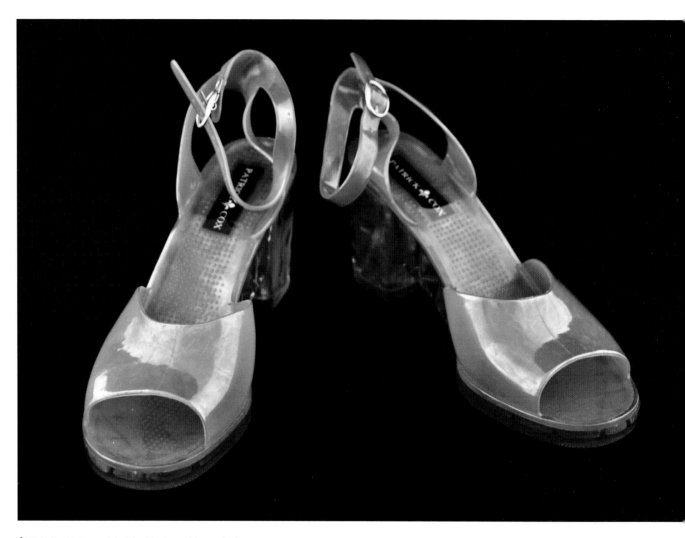

ABOVE: Patrick Cox exploited the injection molding production methods that gave the world the jelly sandal, and he produced a lively range of sandals from clear plastic to the brightest of colors, such as this orange. The design was fun for street and leisurewear.

ABOVE: A black sequinned cover, scattered with purple, red, and silver sequin petals rests on a stiletto of Schiaparelli pink. This description may give an impression of vulgarity, but this shoe is gorgeous and very glamorous.

LEFT: Steffi Graf, Wimbledon champion, is perfectly balanced on her Adidas sports footwear. The soles, thick and bouncy, are wrapped over the shank and toe box, giving protection and support to her foot.

BELOW: Gortex have an established reputation for outdoor wear, clothes for hiking, camping, and mountaineering. They produced this chunky trainer that seems to incorporate all ergonomic principles. The shoe is curved for rhythmical movement, there are Airtex gussets for ventilation, and a ridged sole for grip.

RIGHT: Reebok emerged as a major contender in sports footwear. This trainer is colorful and decorative, pleasing to women wearers who wanted the comfort of an ergonomic structure but with a feminine touch.

More and more women were involved with competitive sports, and manufacturers supplied trainers, many making exaggerated claims for their unique ergonomic designs. Women's boots were produced for climbing and hiking. Steffi Graf and Martina Hingis were wowing the tennis world with their fit, muscular bodies; women envied their strength and supple athleticism, and took note that these girls wore springy, proper sports shoes.

Nike and Adidas continued to refine sports footwear but their trainers faced competition from Puma and Reebok, and copycat versions were now everywhere. They came with glitter trim or suede with silver leather appliqued in speed lines. They also came with heavy soles and Velcro fastenings or in light and elegant designs with lacing.

Another ergonomic footwear manufacturer, Masai Barefoot Technology or MBT, made curved heelless soles so that the foot rocked from heel to toe. This was supposed to imitate the true motion of the bare foot walking. MBT designs for women were chunky Baby Janes with a double cross bar. Seekers of health and comfort loved them.

LEFT: Red or Dead, the oddly named British manufacturer, presented this romantic sandal with its repetitive heart motif. It recalls the dolly bird look of the '60s, girlish in appearance and with a short chunky heel but the shaped toe, following the line of the toes, is pure '90s.

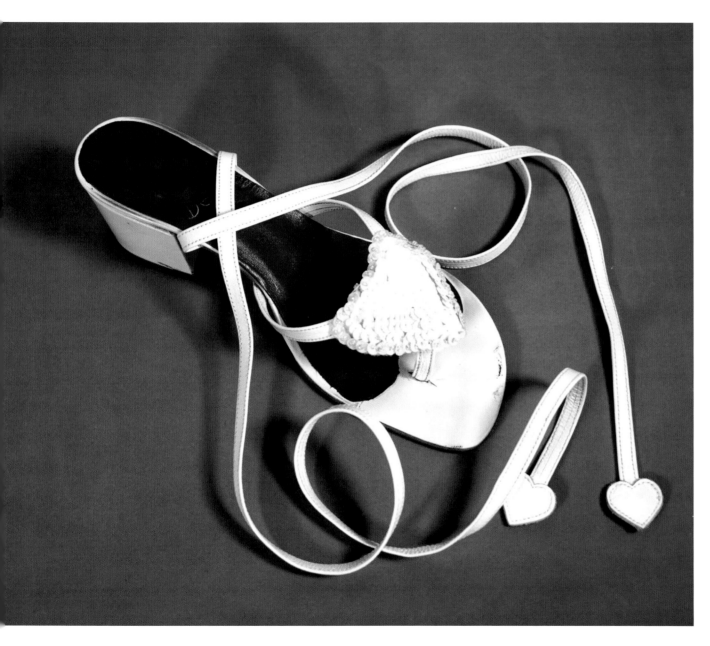

However, the fashion world rose above clunky, sensible footwear. Aware of the throbbing club scene where the young danced and stomped the night away, manufacturers made platforms with ankle straps and sequins, bright colors or floral patterns. Clubbers saw such footwear in the film *Dirty Dancing* (which was set in the 1960s), and they wanted those shoes. In London Vivienne Westwood created subversive designs for wild youth. A suggestive design in fur was too rude for a normal outing and her platforms were impossibly exaggerated, even causing the model Naomi Campbell to fall over when she wore them. Other designers made blue denim platform wedgies or revived the dreaded oxford platform.

Manolo Blahnik gave the fashionistas his Campari, a shoe with a slender heel set into the arch and a long toe with a cross bar placed low against the toes. This design continues to be bought for its sexy, curved silhouette. A shoe from Jimmy Choo exposed the toes below a thick velvet band, while another had studded crystals on swishy high-heeled straps. Both Jimmy Choo and Manolo Blahnik were rocketed to global fame when their footwear appeared in the TV phenomenon *Sex and the City*.

Other designers fought for similar global coverage in the high-end market. However, footwear retail was filled with cheap copies of Fendi, Chanel, Miu Miu, Jimmy Choo, Manolo Blahnik, and Nike. Main street stores showed shelf upon shelf of glitter platforms, wispy strapped high-heeled sandals, and shoes with glass baubles on plastic covers. Trainers appeared in every possible variation, as did mannish loafers and patterned loafers.

ABOVE: The heel remained important throughout the '90s, and it was high and sassy. Here, colored sequins—in marked contrast to the simplicity of the rest of the shoe—draw attention to the heel.

RIGHT: This shoe has a distinctive hollowed heel, and the applique work softens the overall chunky shape. It was the desired accessory for flared, above-the-knee skirts, or bootcut jeans.

LEFT: Jimmy Choo proudly displays one of his designs. He is in his London studio, where a portrait of Diana, Princess of Wales smiles across the tools of his trade. She was his most prestigious customer and helped secure his position among the world's top shoe designers.

BELOW: The heel is high, and the strap doesn't pretend to hold the foot but has a long loose tie as it swings over a naked arch. The sandal has a fabric cover.

LEFT: Jimmy Choo is loved for his airy alluring shoes, like this black grosgrain design. Decorative straps and a diamante buckle transform this court shoe into very chic footwear.

Jimmy
Choo

This designer was born into a Chinese-Malaysian family of cordwainers, and started making shoes as a child. He studied at the Cordwainers College in London and then the London College of Fashion. So it was in London that he opened his own studio in 1988, and his work was celebrated in an eight-page feature in *Vogue*. After her divorce from the Prince of Wales, Lady Diana became his most high-profile client, but it was the crucial role his shoes played in the TV series *Sex in the City* that catapulted him to global fame.

Jimmy Choo opened a company with a partner in 1996, but sold his share in 2001. He now concentrates on his couture and ready-to-wear products, but also works as a bespoke shoemaker in London. He has won many awards for his designs and has been appointed a professor at the University of the Arts in London.

LEFT: Here Jimmy Choo makes a brilliant and original statement. His mules are covered in blue and gold brocade, but each one has a distinctive pattern and are not, as expected, identical.

Wedgie espadrilles and jelly sandals reappeared. Ethnic fabric pumps with rubber soles continued to be imported from the Far East and India: they were covered in sequins and embroidery, and made pretty party shoes, easy on dancing feet. Newer designs were given a totally sequined cover in bright pinks, pearl, and turquoise.

BELOW: After an Italian manufacturer named his wooden high-heeled mules "Candies" he increased sales for them in the U.S. This version of the traditional Italian mule has a sleek high heel wedged into the top of the long shank, making the silhouette more sophisticated than earlier products.

RIGHT: Manolo Blahnik created high-heeled court shoes with printed covers of delicate flower and foliage motifs, then he added a ribbon. The high street copyists responded quickly, making this shoe of similar cover, and adorned with a slanted ribbon, but these pumps came with a tiny blue kitten heel.

Footwear was not chosen because it was appropriate. Boots were worn with lace skirts and trainers with tweed pants. Horse riding influenced the best designs in boots. Women riders including HRH Princess Anne (now the Princess Royal) were much admired, and watching their performances was a television highlight at the Olympic Games. Hermès and Ralph Lauren were among the best craftsmen of riding boots, and they retailed tailored leather fashion boots with minimal decoration.

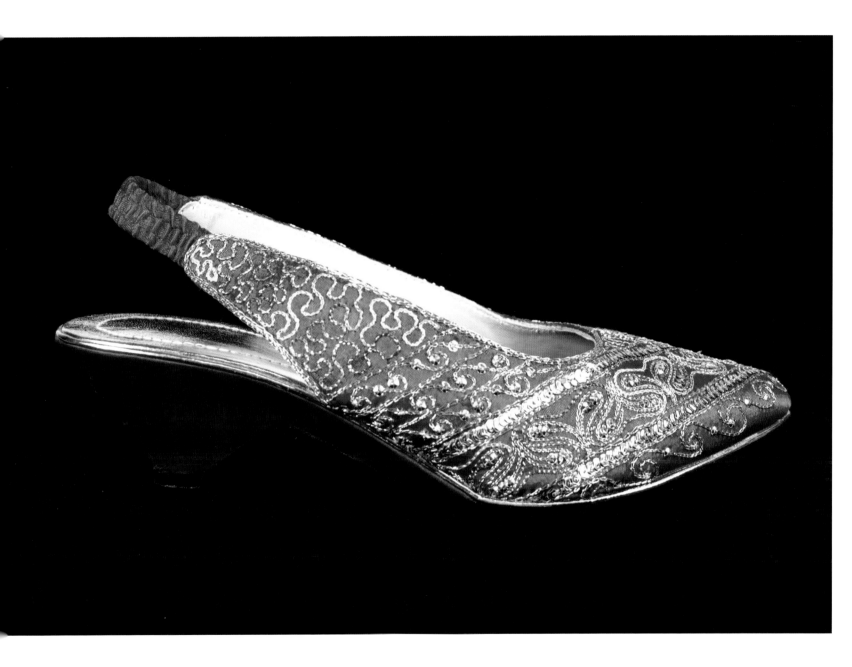

LEFT: The passion for intricate Asian designs and glitter persisted and, in the '90s, shimmering sling-backs such as this were worn with jeans, to go dancing in clubs, and for street wear. The Asian slipper has been modernized: the embroidery is machine stitched, and a small triangular heel adds a little oomph to the old slipper design.

Boots, ankle boots, and sneakers could be seen everywhere and no longer carried seasonal significance. *Vogue* showed models in swimsuits with unlaced boots adorning their feet. Flat sandals were worn in the street and in the evening. They came with twisted leather flowers or rhinestones, in gold or silver leather, and in plaited leather with straps tied numerous times around the ankle. In cities across Europe and Asia, shoppers and tourists of both sexes strode about in their trainers.

There was no prevailing style. The cheap shoe factories in the Far East copied every European and American trend and then flooded the market. At last even the poorest could afford swanky stylish shoes, but the Western shoe industry faced a catastrophe. The names of well-established manufacturers disappeared or were swallowed up in global conglomerates. Clarks had been established in England since 1828 but was forced to relocate to Brazil and India. Florsheim, a household name in the U.S., struggled through the 1990s then moved production to India.

LEFT: This extraordinary design comes from Alexander McQueen, a designer who set out to radicalize clothing. The odd angles and the wide cutouts are forerunners of the strapped, cutaway "barrette" type shoe that was to dominate the next decade, but the heel has not been repeated in the popular main street market.

ABOVE: The British department store, Debenhams, retailed this black sandal. The asymmetrical arrangement of straps made a distinctive, but pleasing, style.

BELOW: Although trainers were appreciated as light and flexible, not all women liked their bulky appearance. The simple unfussiness of these Deja shoes, also designed on anatomical principles, was a great alternative.

RIGHT: Clarks established a niche market in middle range but quality, shoes that were fashionable, but not exhibitionist. These medium stacked heels and the mannish loafer style made the wine colored shoes popular accessories to pants and narrow, short-skirted office suits.

Clarks

Two Quaker brothers, Cyrus and James Clark, began making wool slippers in 1828 from a workshop in Somerset, England. In 1866 the company moved into men's footwear. It was a progressive company, importing equipment from the U.S. and ensuring good conditions for its workers. Its shoes were designed on anatomical theories, and in the 1920s it made perforated and openwork shoes for children and women.

For the next fifty years Clarks supplied the children of Britain with shoes. In the 1950s and 1960s it had successes with its desert boot for men and a leisure shoe, the Wallabee, based on the design of a moccasin. The company also maintained steady sales in quality women's shoes. Along with other major companies, Clarks found itself under siege from Asian manufacturers and in the 1990s moved production to Brazil and India. It acquired the German company Elefanten in 2001, but all the British factories have now been closed.

LEFT: Stylish and cheerful, these wedgies were marketed throughout the high streets of Britain as summerwear. Shoppers considering this shoe were persuaded to buy them because trustworthy Clarks was the manufacturer.

BELOW: The *cendrillon*, or ballet pump, never lost its popularity even when it fell out of fashion. Clarks manufactured many old favorites and knew this patent leather ballet pump would always have a steady market.

The consequence of this was a widening gap between the rich and the less rich. High-end manufacturers and designers determined to make their shoes more and more elite and exclusive. It was a crowded market, yet fashion magazines promoted these shoes without blushing at the prices demanded. The media presented a constant stream of photographs showing well-shod celebrity women or celebrity wives.

Jimmy Choo handcrafts his footwear, and Lady Diana, no longer married to her shorter prince, bought his slender high heels. Chanel and new entrants like Miu Miu made ready-to-wear shoes, their designs growing more extravagant as promotion projects brought them high visibility and, consequently, desirability.

RIGHT: This design from Stella McCartney almost defies description. The high heel and tight, narrow shank hint at fetishism, of shoes that make movement difficult. They have a lovely mix of elements—the transparent vamp, the zigzag stitching down the heel, and long straps threaded through rings on the vamp then pulled up to be wrapped around the leg. This is a luxury shoe, disdainful of utility.

LEFT: An Italian manufacturer has created a high triangular heel, and trimmed the throat of this black patent shoe with a tiny cord of pink. The cover is cut in curves to reveal the arch, and cunningly crafted petals and leaves reveal a glimpse of toes in the cut away toe box. The shoe announces its fine craftsmanship in defiance of cheap imports.

RIGHT: Emma Hope finds her inspiration in Renaissance and medieval design, and much of her work involves embroidered, soft, slipper-like shoes. The vamp of her soft suede, boudoir mule has a familiar cut, glimpsed, perhaps, on the foot of a nobleman in a sixteenth century painting.

Christian Louboutin made Lucite platforms, which were transparent but with red petals embedded in the heels. Emma Hope, a new English designer, made velvet pumps similar to old-fashioned men's slippers. She decorated mules, and her shoes were embroidered, beaded, and exclusive. As the decade drew to its close, the house of Versace favored heavy straps, wound high up the calf, on stiletto heels. The shoes had the sinister look of bondage footwear seen in the fetish magazines.

Shoes had long ceased to represent a particular outlook. Gender equality and female independence were no longer major issues, while glamour and fashion had re-claimed women's interest. The non-rich continued to buy cheap copies but, thanks to the endorsement of elite footwear by celebrities, they were aware that these did not have the status of really well-made shoes.

LEFT: This shoe would add immense glamour to any outfit. The rich blue satin and the long sequinned vamp add a subtle allure to a design that already displays a sexy stiletto. The design is confident and luxurious.

2000s
DREAMS AND DELUSIONS

The new millennium opened with optimism. A thriving economy meant the good life for one and all. The struggle for gender equality and battles against racial discrimination had been won, and the dreams of a peaceful multi-cultural tolerance seemed to have been realized. Western society was democratized and, it was assumed, that now each citizen could realize their full potential.

For many, this was a permit for total individualism. Even the fashion world abandoned ideas of rigor and standards; they named a pop star known as Lady Gaga among the best-dressed women in the world, while a leading British newspaper gave her the Wonkiest Wardrobe award. Her shoes are as eccentric as the rest of her gear. But the fashionistas were happy now to recognize the individual above *haut couture*.

RIGHT: Lady Gaga revives the weirdly high platforms of the 1960s Rock 'n' Rollers. A child of the decade, famous for bizarre dressing and stage presentation, she has a ghostly figure draped on her piano as she stomps that heavy shoe to the rhythm. This was a stage show in New York.

Reality television shows gave ordinary people the chance to be a celebrity; fame was not confined to the talented few. Global communication on the world-wide-web meant any individual could find an audience for their ideas, writings, and art. Public appearances and photographs on the web gave many the opportunity to wear bold clothes and gorgeous shoes from Louboutin or Puma or Fendi. But, of course, these things also caused competition for publicity and encouraged more and more bizarre wardrobes in a bid to attract attention.

RIGHT: Entertainers moved theatrical costume off the stage and wore the clothes to celebrity events. These sparkling and cleverly crafted shoes have no shank so the heel is pushed against the toes. Lady Gaga wore them at an award ceremony in California—but, it was reported, she changed them soon after her grand arrival.

Stella McCartney referred to seventeenth century slap-shoes when she designed this footwear. They are constructed from canvas and metal, and they are stamped as "suitable for vegetarians." Whether this makes them easier to wear is open to doubt, but then these shoes are not made for walking but for serious status.

Multiculturalism was dealt a bitter blow when religious fanatics destroyed the Twin Towers in New York. Consequently a marked fear of other cultures began to underlie political debate. The gentle insistence of the early environmentalist became the angry voice of the eco-warrior. Well organized and clever at spreading their fears, the new environmentalists became a global organization. But unlike the hippies, they did not readily abandon the comforts of modernity, preferring to harness technology to carry their message.

BELOW: This ergonomically designed sandal resembles machinery and is a minor miracle of technology. Velcro-strapped, ventilated, with its rubber sole curved and studded, it insists on health and comfort. The makers, Footjoy, claim it would serve as a golf shoe, but golfers have certain codes of dressing and it is unlikely these sandals would be welcome on the green.

BELOW: This is a golf shoe from Footjoy, and it fits all conventions of the well-dressed player. Made of leather, it is front-lacing and resembles the traditional spectator shoe. The sole is studded and is shaped for maximum foot comfort and flexibility.

LEFT: Trainers rule the world! The comfort of this athletic footwear, made of easily cleaned synthetic fabrics, have made them the favorite of many people. The majority of men and women on this demonstration for a safe environment are wearing trainers. There are, of course, fashions in shape and color and some makes have more status than others, but trainers of any sort are standard wear.

BELOW: Injection molding revolutionized shoe manufacture. This flexible sandal is a single piece of shaped plastic. It is made by Croc, and shows an advance in design from the first clumsy sandals molded by this production method.

At huge demonstrations, the warriors of both sexes wore their trainers and aerodynamic sports shoes, all manufactured from high tech fabrics. The Vivo Barefoot was the newest offering in the manufacture of shoes, scientifically researched and made of malleable synthetic fabrics. Made by Terra Plana, this shoe had a puncture-resistant ultra thin sole designed to replicate as closely as possible the natural, healthy movement of bare feet.

The Croc was another great new success. Made of plastic, it is durable and washable. It is a clog, with holes punched into the cover. Comfortable and easy to wear, Crocs come in many colors and sell in huge numbers. For those who want to add a flourish, plastic flowers, designed to slot into the cover holes, are available.

ABOVE: The classic court shoe, associated with craftsmanship and high-end elegance, were available at very low prices across main street. These were retailed by New Look, a bargain-clothing store in Britain.

The noble attempt to open access to money and home ownership to a huge number of people proved a Bad Thing. The system of easy credit for all turned into a deep global hole of debt, creating widespread unemployment, and many bankruptcies. Frightened by economic recession, many women appreciated the availability of cheap shoes from Asia.

Designs were interesting and quality was much improved. Some unexpected footwear was on offer, for instance, trainers were given heels, the manufacturers recognizing the trend for laced front sports shoes, while relenting to a feminine longing for sexy high heeled footwear.

BELOW: This is the decade that ignored social and design conventions—a delight to shoppers who now could find something, somewhere to their taste. Not quite a sandal, not quite a pump, this shoe has a gleam, known as "gun metal," a wide peep-toe and a tiny kitten heel. It is stamped Anne Taylor Loft, an American manufacturer.

With reference to the '50s, ballet pumps and Baby Dolls returned to the catwalk. These Baby Doll shoes with short, rounded toes and very high straight heels are very flattering. They give the illusion of small feet and high arches. Designers adorned them with bows on the vamp, or lined the edge of the cover with a contrasting color. These new Baby Dolls came in shiny materials and popsicle colors.

The shape—that is, the short toe and the high heel—was retained but sometimes, a peep toe was added, or the cover was lavishly decorated with colored leather flowers, or plastic if the shoe was made in a synthetic fabric. But there was also a revival in long, squared-off toes. This design was found in strappy high heels or elegant court shoes, often adorned with a buckle on the cover.

RIGHT: This shoe recalls the heyday of Hollywood glamour, of Monroe, Mansfield, and Bette Davis wearing wildly sexy outfits. The very high heel, the short toe, and a red bow matched with leopard skin print epitomized luxury and money, but this shoe is made of plastic and retails at a low price on the high street.

BELOW: Kitten heels and decorative touches were popular, worn with jeans or short skirts. The cut-leather flower on the vamp has a stone pinned to its center, a small confirmation that this shoe is organic and made of leather.

LEFT: Christian Louboutin attends an event to honor his position as a leading designer. The occasion was the Christian Louboutin Cocktail and it was held in Berlin in 2010. Here he cuddles one of his greatly desirable creations.

ABOVE: Louboutin is part of a movement that perceives fashion as an art form, rather than a craft. His beautiful shoes, such as this one, show imagination and creativity with a fine sense of color balance, but the shoe is decorative. Delicious as an ornament for the feet, unfortunately, it is not practical footwear.

Christian
Louboutin

BELOW: A gorgeous variation on the boot shoe, this gives the old style a very high heel and extends the pointed toe. It is made of synthetic pink-ringed lizard skin, and Louboutin has stamped his name on his signature scarlet sole.

Christian Louboutin has said that, as a boy in Paris, he would sneak off to watch the cabaret showgirls. He loved their costumes and especially their high-heeled shoes. He left school early, determined to become a shoemaker. After training with Charles Jourdan he opened his own workshop in Paris in 1991.

Louboutin liked the theatrical, and his designs show this preference. He re-introduced the stiletto heel, which was almost five inches high, and used glossy materials to make narrow-vamped sexy shoes. The under-soles of his footwear are painted a distinctive bright red, and on select designs, the heel leaves an imprint of a rosette: these he describes as "Follow Me" shoes. Louboutin likes to emphasize the arches, thinking it is the sexiest part of a woman's foot. Madonna, Nicole Kidman, and Angelina Jolie are among his clients as is Sarah Jessica Parker, the star of *Sex in the City*.

RIGHT: There were shoes made for "art" and celebrity displays but, of course, the shops carried lovely, crafted and wearable footwear. This pair of charming sandals from the couture designer Roland Cartier, has a slender, medium height heel, and a neatly tied bow on the vamp. It is sexy but easy to wear.

The strongest trend was towards boot-shoes. In these, the cover reached to the ankle, and the heel was high but sturdy. The shoe was peep toed and carried a zipped opening on the side or down the center of the cover. In the more *outré* designs, the cover would open like the petals of a flower around the ankle.

ABOVE: The classic court shoe will always find its place in a woman's shoe rack. This crocodile skin has its own distinctive appearance and comes with an elongated shank and long, blunted toe. It carries the stamp of the U.S. designer, Michelle D.

The movie star, Gwyneth Paltrow wowed the crowd at a red carpet event when she wore a very high mini skirt accessorized with bare legs and a brutal pair of high heeled boot-shoes. Bare legs, for long considered unsightly except with summer frocks and sandals, became the norm among models in this decade.

New names came onto the footwear scene. The designers, Azagury and Clergerie found favor among the fashionistas.

LEFT: Louboutin's distinctive soles confirm that these shoes are his creation. The shank is steep, the vamp has vanished, making way for the toe box. The design can only be described as very feminine gladiator sandals. They were displayed on the feet of movie star, Gwyneth Paltrow, when she attended a premier in Los Angeles.

RIGHT: This picture reveals the importance of celebrity endorsement to shoe manufacturers and designers. The star, Charlotte Gainsbourg, posing on the red carpet, ensures a market for the shoes she is wearing. It is an elite market, but manufacturers in Asia are quick to produce variations of famous designers, thus delivering celebrity style to the popular market.

LEFT: These black patent leather sandals have a T-bar threaded through loops on the cut-away arch, then attached to an ankle strap. A metal chain defines the heel. The designer of this sandal, Versace, favors very high showgirl heels.

High-heeled sandals appeared with thick bands folded across the arch, then turned round the ankle and held with a large buckle. Colors were pearly or brilliant: technology allowed a wild choice, and animal fur patterns became very popular. Shoes in every style came in red leopard skin, red zebra, or pink crocodile and were abundant in the stores. Gold and silver glitter also sold fast.

LEFT: This sling-back high heel has a balanced silhouette and is a very pleasing shoe. The faux leopard skin lining is a nice touch. The short platform sole is very contemporary. This design is retailed through Next, a British main street chain, proving that there is a big market for glamorous, very high-heeled shoes.

Versace's slave sandal look, first revealed in the late '90s, also became a prominent fashion theme. Very similar to late nineteenth century sandal-boots, the cover hid the toe, but then it was taken to mid-calf where it was cut out to achieve a thick, strapped effect. Punk type rivets or buckles ran down the outer leg. Again the heels were very high, and the effect is very sexy. The fashionistas found beautifully crafted versions from Chanel, Louboutin, Azagury, and Fendi, but main street stores also had their own, much cheaper, versions.

RIGHT: The wedge is curved to recall a Louis heel and the cover is cut high to hold a loop for the ankle strap. These details create a balanced, well-designed sandal retailed by Marks and Spencer, the British department store.

BELOW: A much-loved design was re-issued by Liz Claiborne. Plaited string and a fabric cover are familiar elements taken from the traditional espadrille, and this stylish wedgie will always find a ready market.

Technology also allowed a redesign of the platform. Now, instead of the platform filling the sole against the toes, the platform is smaller than the sole, and its sides slope inwards, so the foot seems perched in airy fashion above the sole. Color combinations are imaginative, with the platform contrasting with the cover, and the heel given a third color. Rock stars, such as the group Girls Aloud, compete to be fashionistas rather than shocking with their clothes, and float into nightclubs and film premiers on these airy platforms. Wealth and status are keynotes in footwear.

LEFT: This shaped wedge heel is very high, and there is no platform to help the foot lie easy. On the contrary, the foot's exposed arch is deeply curved and erotic. The gleaming leather and woven vamp, revealing the toes, add to the mood. The sandal comes from the U.S.

RIGHT: The pop group, Girls Aloud, perform in London and their shoes reveal a lack of fashion consensus and reveal the enormous variety of footwear available in the shoe stores. Between them the Girls are sporting high vamped sling-backs, ankle boots, neo-barrettes, and court shoes.

Boots are perennial favorites, and come, as does all other footwear, in a great variety of designs and colors. *Haut couture* houses promote thigh high boots matched with short skirts. The boots gleam with patent leather, or are flesh colored suede. They are laced up the sides, or decorated with heavy zips. These are not snapped up on main street, but the comfortable and yes, ugly, Ugg boot has become a great success.

A traditional Australian design, the Ugg is a simply cut and folded mid-calf boot made from sheepskin. The wool is folded inside. The wonderful quality of sheepskin is that it cools in the sun and warms in the winter. Australian surfers as well as farmers wore these boots. A manufacturer, Brian Smith, registered Ugg as a trademark in 1978, but the style took off as a fashion item in the 2000s. Now, it can be seen worn with floaty summer skirts or long woolen coats and, of course, there are copies to be found in all the stores.

RIGHT: This is tall, elegant, and commanding, carrying the air of a Victorian military boot. The toe is blunt and a buckle adds authority. It is an American product and sold to the higher end of the market.

ABOVE: The Ugg boot has been described as clumpy, even ugly but its simple unassuming shape can be assimilated with soft skirts as easily as with jeans. The Ugg is also extremely warm in the cold but cools in the heat, and lots of women are grateful for the comfort of the Ugg.

RIGHT: The soft, crumpled leather of this cowboy boot by Justin gives it an authentic air of horse riding and the great outdoors. The tooled leather follows the traditional markings of early cowboy boots.

Bally

The Swiss Carl Franz Bally started a company selling ribbons and elastic webbing to shoemakers in 1851. It is claimed he went to Paris and bought a stock of shoes, and this led him to the manufacture of footwear. After his death his son continued the business, concentrating on high quality shoes. Bally was a company that produced conventional designs, bought by the large number of women who were less interested in fashion than in elegance and tradition.

The company survived the Depression and World War II, and until the 1990s enjoyed worldwide sales and a reputation for craftsmanship. As the global production of shoes expanded, other companies challenged Bally's position as a leader in classic footwear. In 1999 the company was sold to an American investment firm who are determined to regain Bally's reputation and former market position.

ABOVE: This neat pump cannot offend anyone and will please many. It is feminine and promises comfort while flattering the foot. It is typical of Bally's careful design history, and was commissioned by Dolcis.

BELOW: The company, fearing its old conventional style was moribund, gave creative director Brian Atwood free reign when he was appointed early in the decade. These sandals use organic materials and are bold in design, but quality has not been compromised.

ABOVE: Brian Atwood, creative designer for Bally, presented these shoes at an event sponsored by the Environmental Media Association in California. The gleaming patent in delicious colors and the new shape of inward sloping platforms confirm Bally's reputation for great, well-made footwear.

Trainers continue to sell to thousands of women. The Williams sisters, Serena and Venus, reinforce respect for this footwear. These remarkable athletes whirl through the world of tennis. They are tall, muscular, fast, and powerful. And the many thousands of women who have taken to jogging, rambling, cycling, and hill climbing take a keen interest in all developments in sports footwear.

LEFT: Here is a glittering array of Joe Sneakers from British designer, Emma Hope. The sneaker design refers to the famous early sportswear, the Converse All-Star, in the thick sole, white toe, and laces, this is a feminine version and does not pretend to be sportswear. Joe Sneakers are fun and sequinned and women of the new millennium are free to wear them shopping or to a nightclub.

LEFT: Athletic footwear has become powerful and chunky, even huge on the foot. Serena and Venus Williams both wear carefully constructed shoes and pay as much attention to the weight, bounce, and hardiness of their footwear as they do to the balance and weight of their racquets.

BELOW: Ageing Baby Boomers understood the value of feet, that part of the body that doesn't put on weight or wrinkle. Extravagant, delicious foot ornament became very important in the 2000s. This American design, marked Moda Spana, fulfills these needs. The combination of color, translucent medium heel, and a feathered decoration, hiding a cluster of crystals, couldn't be prettier.

The baby boomers are in late middle age now, and they are determined to combine fashion with comfort. Fortunately, the fashion world manufactures elegant sports versions with sleek ornament and color. Emma Hope introduced her Joe Sneaker; it has a thick sole, white toe, and laces but actually, it is a narrow elegant sneaker. The difference is the fully sequined cover that brings a girlish glamour to the traditional tennis shoe. Joe Sneaker comes in a variety of colors, and versions appear with animal print covers. Needless to say, sequined sneakers appear in shoe boutiques everywhere.

BELOW: Mules are high in the ratings for erotic value. This low sloping shank and medium heel make for comfort, but the vamp of glass beads and embroidery is guaranteed to make any foot enchanting.

Young designers long to break into the lucrative footwear market, but the economic recession thwarts their ambition. The established names—Christian Louboutin, Chanel, Fendi, and others of that ilk—fight to stay at the top. Their efforts are supported by Kylie Minogue, an entertainer with a love of extravagance: her musical shows are pantomimes of glitz and glamour. Kylie is a pop fashion icon and in tune with *Vogue* magazine when it proclaims that "no adornment is too much."

BELOW: There is nothing like the mule! Sleek, glamorous, sexy—no wonder they have been worn for centuries. This version has gold and pink brocade on the vamp and heel. The vamp is held within swirling silver lines and the result is an adorable little mule.

LEFT: Christian Louboutin returns to the exclusive territory where fashion equals art. This extravaganza of sequins, lace, bare toes, and buckles is a mix of creative design and splendid craftsmanship, but it stands in the rarefied atmosphere of the untouchable. Here it is on display at media event in Berlin, Germany, a fashionable center for cutting edge art.

LEFT: Kylie Minogue performs in the splendor of a short silver tutu with pom-poms stuck in her hair. Her shoes, also silver, are jazzed up slave sandals. The platform soles are set away from the welt and slope inwards, a design that eases the wearer's movement in such very high heels—as Kylie favors. Short women like Kylie enjoy the added height such footwear gives them.

RIGHT: The singer, Beyonce pairs a dark tuxedo style suit with her colorful Balenciaga shoes. They are complex in design, with triangles of color set into the vamp, and a swathe of blue leather wrapping around the top of the heel. Additionally, there is an extravagant, high counter of yellow and red.

285

To prove the point, it shows Prada's velvet shoes thick with metal studs. The magazine photographs a shoe with a green, netted leather cover, caught at the ankle by broad bows of blue suede. Designed by Balenciaga, this confection is perched on transparent acrylic shrunken platforms. Balmain produces a high-heeled boot with a decorative wide zipper spiraling from arch to mid-calf.

RIGHT: The pop singer Rihanna, proves that the dress has become accessory to the shoe. Attending a radio interview in New York, her dark short outfit is scarcely memorable but no one could forget the footwear. These Balanciaga gladiator boots were launched in spring '08.

ABOVE: A smooth silver surface is the cover for this sophisticated sandal. The curves of the cut-away vamp are repeated in curved cut-aways on the heel. A small bauble of beads encircling a faux pearl adds an extra touch to the classy, narrow heeled sandal. The footwear is labelled Touch Up and, in all likelihood, was manufactured in a developing country.

Jimmy Choo makes thigh high boots in black and white pony skin, while silver boot-sandals on stiletto heels glitter with big studs of Swarovski crystal. Louis Vuitton designs a platform with a peep toe, and a thick ankle strap of velvet ribbon. The entire shoe is made of molded lace, and the heel further decorated with pearls.

LEFT: Jimmy Choo maintains the airiness that marks his style even as he designs a high fitting vamp to this sandal. The decoration, too, confirms Choo as a man who understands pattern and color.

LEFT: The high street fashion store, H&M, retained the Jimmy Choo company to produce a range for their stores. These strapped and studded sandal shoes appeared at the opening presentation, proving that the cut-away style was popular with many shoppers.

ABOVE: The profile is demure and evokes the familiar Baby Jane design, with its low heel and cross bar.

BELOW: The silver inner sole is marked with the distinctive flourish of Robert Clergerie's signature that also serves as his trademark.

BELOW: This shoe from Clergerie has a demure, intellectual air. Yes, the Baby Jane air is childish but here the apron vamp and the squared toe make this a serious accessory for a stylish but private individual. It is this quality of dignity, as opposed to exhibitionism, that defines Clergerie.

Robert
Clergerie

The French designer Robert Clergerie studied commerce as a young man, later becoming an accountant and real estate agent. This background gave him the confidence to seek a managerial position for Charles Jourdan. He won the job, and went on discover an interest in shoes.

Clergerie bought the French shoe company Unic in 1977. In 1981 he launched his own collection and within a few years was winning awards from the shoe industry, especially for his architecturally designed heels. He opened his own retail stores, but about one-third of his sales are through other outlets in the U.S. Although he is known for his luxury designs, he manufactures for the middle market under the brand name Espace. His son shares his interest in footwear and organises the Salon Première Classe, a shoe exhibition that coincides with the bi-annual Prêt-a-Porter collections in Paris.

RIGHT: Robert Clergerie surrounded by his shoes poses in his studio in Paris. Now over '70 years old, he has won many awards and accolades for his contribution to the footwear industry.

There is no end to the imaginative designs brought by the possibilities of modern materials. Celebrities and high-level fashion magazines promote this footwear, and glamourous girls appear in the weirdest and best shoe designs. At the Academy Awards ceremony (aka the Oscars) and film premiers, millions of TV viewers survey these women as they glide up the red carpet. Viewers have critical and envious eyes: shoes are sumptuous and dramatic; shoes define Woman as daring and wildly sexual.

LEFT: Until the twentieth century, the great mass of working people were condemned to clumsy, often ugly footwear. Now, a girl can run up to town and find an adorable silver sandal at very little cost. This was manufactured the English company, Ravel.

ABOVE: Holiday sandals, in a color mix that Ferragamo might envy, are sold by Wal-Mart, the huge U.S. retail, low-price company.

LEFT: Every woman who adores shoes maintains a love affair with mules, and this silver pair has a charming clutch of straps, caught in a skinny bow on the vamp. They are stamped Esino.

BELOW: This shoe keeps all the elements of a classic court shoe but has moved beyond even the high standards of that essential design. The combination of dusty pink suede and silver, and a restrained frill on the vamp, make a stunning appearance. This superb shoe can be found in every good department store.

BELOW: Ever since Ferragamo introduced his wedgie in the 1940s it has remained a firm favorite. This sandal also recalls another early tradition—that of a cut-out vamp (as opposed to straps). This is a very attractive wedgie made by the Chinese Laundry shoe manufacturer in the U.S.

Ecologists remind consumers constantly of environmental concerns and the desperate need to control global warming, but manufacturers across Asia are reluctant to curtail production. Technology has brought wealth to once poor rural populations. Western consumers, struggling with recession, are reluctant to stop buying cheap footwear.

BELOW: A very old method of making footwear is used in this sandal. The toe knob was known in India centuries before Christ, but the sequins and the arch strap are modern innovations. The sandal has a leather sole.

The longing to appear fashionable, to own shoes that imply status and financial success drives, as it always has, women to buy gorgeous shoes. The truth, however, is that the shoe worn by the largest number of people, the shoe with the biggest sales in the whole wide world, is the rubber and plastic flip-flop, the modern throwback to the thong footwear first worn by the Ancients.

RIGHT: The flip-flop is the footwear that beats all others, be they ergonomic wonders or gorgeous frivolities from top designers. This, probably the first ever shoe design but now made in modern materials of rubber and plastic, is manufactured mainly in China and millions of pairs are sold every day across the world.

BELOW: Flip-flops are so easy to wear and to make, which makes them popular. But they are usually just plastic and rubber. Here is a zippy little design dripping with gems and crystals, perfect for a hot, hot evening at an outdoor café on the beach.

Novelty Shoes
Fanciful footwear

The erotic delight of feet, enfolded by soft leather and pretty straps, is not a strange, modern pleasure. In the *Old Testament* book of *Ecclesiastes*, a man sighs, "How beautiful are thy feet with shoes." From the start of shoe wearing, shoes have been designed to enhance the eroticism of the foot.

The Lotus shoes of China are probably the earliest known examples of shoes with no practical use except to add sensuality to a woman's foot. The shoes are tiny because, for centuries, Chinese girls born into important families had their feet bound and deliberately deformed so they could not walk, but only totter a few steps. The belief that small feet are erotic is persistent: 88% of modern women consistently buy shoes too small for them.

LEFT: This footwear utterly ignores the anatomy and allure of the female foot. It represents an obsession with radical design concepts, and comes from the designer, once *enfant terrible* of fashionable London circles, the late Alexander McQueen.

BELOW: The passionate color and exquisite embroidery is a cruelly inappropriate ornament for a woman whose feet have been deliberately crippled. The delicacy of this shoe, which is about four inches long, is devised for a woman who cannot walk easily through her own home —and certainly cannot run away.

RIGHT: This coy Edwardian lady promises pain as pleasure, and her high, tightly laced boots demand that her victim prolong the session by undertaking the task of unlacing these very boots.

BELOW: Would the secretary of the golf club be pleased to see these wooden clogs rocking across the greens? Westwood chooses to make a witty interpretation of the familiar fringed tongue and spikes of golfing footwear. She stitches the tongue to the vamp and cuts an angular chunk out of the very deep curved wooden sole.

RIGHT: When the highly experienced and professional model, Naomi Campbell, wore these on the catwalk, she wobbled and fell to the floor. But the design has been lauded as an art piece and samples are now displayed in museums. This green version is in the Northampton Shoe Museum, England.

Vivienne
Westwood

BELOW: This shoe has all the characteristics of the fetish shoe. The arch is cruelly arched, and the heel thrust high. This shoe is kept in the Bath Fashion Museum, England.

Vivienne Westwood was trained at art schools in London, and was part of the Punk movement. Her career as a designer has been a rage against conventional fashion, and her shoes resemble fetish footwear, often carrying exaggerated decoration such as over-large tongues or fur folded in a suggestive manner. Her heels are generally very high.

Westward's influence on *haute couture* has been strong though her footwear is generally purchased by museums or by women rich enough to disregard convention. In 2008, however, a mellower Westwood designed for the Brazilian mass manufacturer Melissa, creating shoes of injection-molded plastic that are pretty, conventional sling-backs with peep toes and a neat heart decoration on the cover. These, in contrast to her other creations, are both wearable and inexpensive.

LEFT: This Japanese noblewoman wears wooden pattens to protect her feet from the snow. Her serving maid wears them, too, although hers seem to be lower. Such a practical design could easily evolve into extreme design to enhance the sex appeal of the feet.

RIGHT: This is the extreme of fetish footwear, shankless and with heels hoisted, rendering the foot completely useless. The woman who puts this shoe on her feet will be in pain and her feet immoveable; she will become a prisoner.

Other shoes designed for erotic purposes share one quality with the binding of feet: the foot is forced into a shape that makes walking difficult if not impossible. Pointy-toed shoes or tall boots are favored. Both styles tip the arch over the toes while the heel is forced upwards on impossibly high heels. Platforms have been exaggerated to absurd heights—Venetian chopins are famous, and similar designs used to be worn in Japan. This exaggeration remains popular in the fetish footwear market. Incapacitated by such footwear, the woman is available for fantasy playacting. Despite the sadomasochism implied by these designs, fashion has incorporated the look—even Chanel has an "S&M" version of her two-tone pump.

Some designers create simply imaginative, unpractical designs. Beth Levine produced a loafer designed to resemble a racing car and Samuel Mazza modeled a staircase to tumble down the inner sole of his mules. Gorgeous designs can be found in theatrical footwear; sandals with molded, realistic toes were made for an opera company, while David Evins made a curious curved wedge covered in rhinestones for the 1935 movie, *Cleopatra*.

Technology allows sensible, flexible materials; ergonomics measures our methods of walking and running. But nothing will replace the crystals, laces, feathers, embroidery, and sequins that make the most delectable shoes. And we will always want and desire frothy, frivolous, sexy, high-heeled shoes.

LEFT: This shoe is an elaborate joke, fooling around with the absurd height of some platform shoes. It was created by a craftsman and was intended as a witty advertising display in a shoe store. It was made in the 1980s.

Thea
Cadabra

In 1973 the British woman Thea Cadabra graduated from university in Turkish and Russian, but did not become an interpreter as she'd intended. Instead she was apprenticed to a Turkish cordwainer in London. In 1975 she moved into her own workshop, and within four short years had won a Crafts Council Shoe Show award.

Thea Cadabra worked in France, where she was employed by Charles Jourdan. She then went on to work as an independent designer in the U.S., before returning to Britain in 2004. By this time she had built a reputation for originality. Her shoes are given a three-dimensional effect with flying wings and folded fabrics rising up from the cover. She fixes colored shapes that turn the footwear into little illustrations or perhaps miniature stage sets. Her inspirations are David Bowie, Biba, and *The Rocky Horror Show*. Museums in Britain, Belgium, and Australia have purchased her work.

LEFT: Somehow, Cadabra's shoes do not fall into the "this-is-art" category of footwear. Her shoes are beautifully crafted and she creates a fantastic decoration for the foot. This is a gorgeous skyscape but the shoe appears wearable and not simply for display.

BELOW: Cadabra uses the softest leather to create her pictures, and her materials suit the foot. This Dragon Shoe One is so original in concept and realization, and is so special a person would be reluctant to over use the footwear for fear of damaging the beast. The shoe falls into that special category—an heirloom object.

RIGHT: The designer calls this her Summer Water Lily Shoe, and indeed brilliant blooms float from a sea of aquamarine. Any foot would become instantly alluring and beautiful shod in this dream of a shoe.

A Visit to the
Cordwainers'
College, London, England

The Cordwainers' College in London is housed in a large, old building, and the first impression is one of high ceilings, swirling corridors and narrow staircases. But these lead to large airy rooms, with modern equipment set up in rows, attended by students absorbed in their craft. There is a busy but relaxed atmosphere, free of intimidation; students, in need of an urgent hint, stop their tutors in passages or the cafeteria in full expectation of careful advice. Inspirational posters showing the work of famous shoe designers line the walls.

The College has recently become part of the University of the Arts London, but has a long history that can be traced back to the historic guild system. It has a high reputation, and includes Jimmy Choo and Emma Hope among its alumumni. Students learn about traditional craft methods, but they are taught, and have access to an impressive range of up-to-date technology.

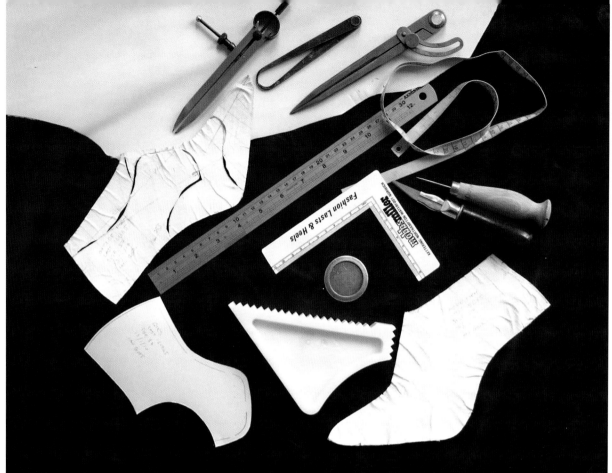

The making of a wooden last is a craft in itself. The craftsman must think how the foot moves inside a shoe. The symmetry of the toes, the height of the big toe must be measured. The width of the foot, and the contour and girth of the instep must be calibrated. The shank must be suited to the heel height because this area takes the weight of the foot in motion. The finished lasts have a beauty often found in handmade products. Sadly, the number of people with last making skills is shrinking.

When the students at the Cordwainers' College start to make a shoe, they are allowed to select from these bins of plastic lasts, filled with every shape and size. The colours are of no technical significance but merely reveal the manufacturer's preference. The students are taught the rudiments of making a wooden last, and can perfect their skills at this job if they wish.

The design and decoration of a shoe may come from inspiration worked through numerous sketches, but, finally, they must be formalised and drawn to accurate measurements. Measuring tools—dividers, a tape and so on—and cutting tools are essential.

When the design sketches have been finalised, measurements have to be confirmed on a last. The design is worked on one size of last. The last is marked with location points, guides for measurements and design. This plastic last has been covered with masking tape that can be peeled off and the last re-used. The shoe design is drawn up as a paper pattern.

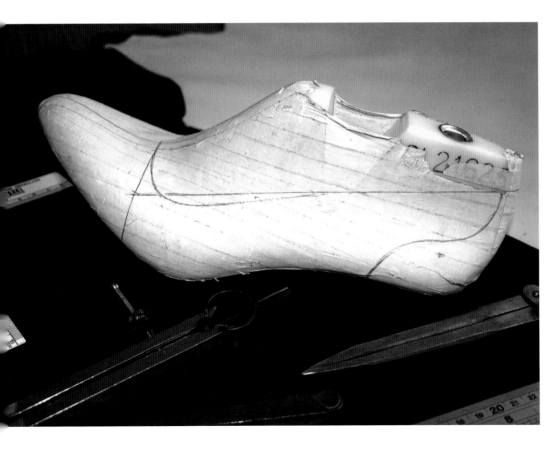

Having ensured accurate measurements, and after matching it against the last, the paper pattern is placed on the leather and cut out using a clicking knife. However, the College has computer software programmed to create and cut the patterns. Students gain an understanding of this specialist Cad Cam software for the shoe industry.

These metal templates are used sometimes to cut the upper pieces. They work like cookie cutters and have sharp edges that, when pressed, using a hydraulic press, cut the leather to shape. They are known, in the trade, as press knives. These templates have not always been in use. Traditionally, cardboard patterns with brass bound edges were used. When cutting the leather with a knife, it would click against these brass edges, hence the leather cutter came to be called the clicker.

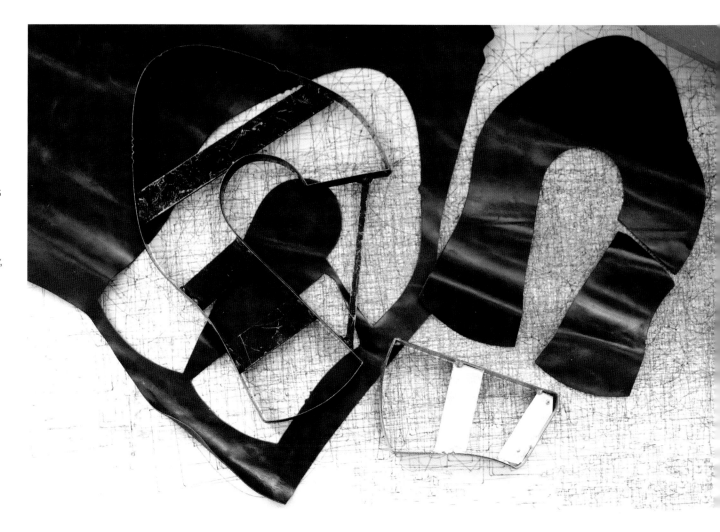

On a sewing machine designed specifically for shoemaking, the cordwainer sews the pieces together, a process known as closing. Here, an elastic gusset is sewn in place. The leather pattern pieces may occasionally be held against the last as a continual check that the work is accurate. Traditionally, women were employed in the closing room.

Traditionally, in most styles of footwear, the sewn upper, or cover would now be nailed on the last. To shape and firm the cover, a toe puff (toe box) and counter stiffener would be inserted between the cover and the last, and hung in a mulling room, a place that is heated and humid to make the leather of the cover malleable. The modern Cordwainer has equipment to speed up this process. The back part moulding equipment allows for the back part to be stretched over an aluminium mould that represents the last shape—the aluminium mould is a negative copy. Later, wiper blades will smooth the bottom cover edges in preparation for the cover to be attached to the insole.

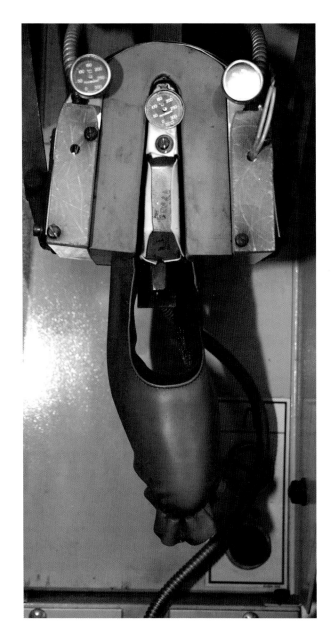

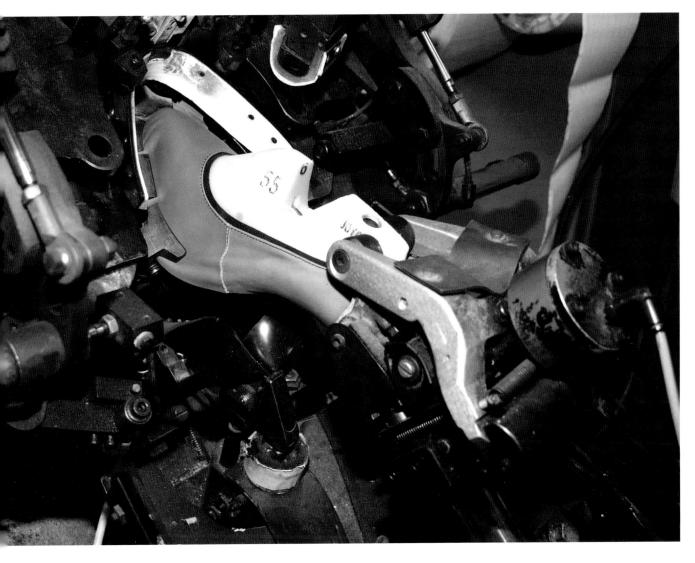

Traditionally the cover, or upper, would remain stretched over the last while it was secured to an insole by adhesive and tacks, and all would be left on the last for a number of days to ensure the shape is retained. This is called cemented construction. The modern Cordwainer uses a heat setting machine to replicate this process in a few minutes.. The heel is processed first, as described on Page 312. Here the machine is stretching and moulding the front of the shoe, then hot melt adhesive is injected onto the insole and wiper plates spread the stretched shoe leather onto the insole.

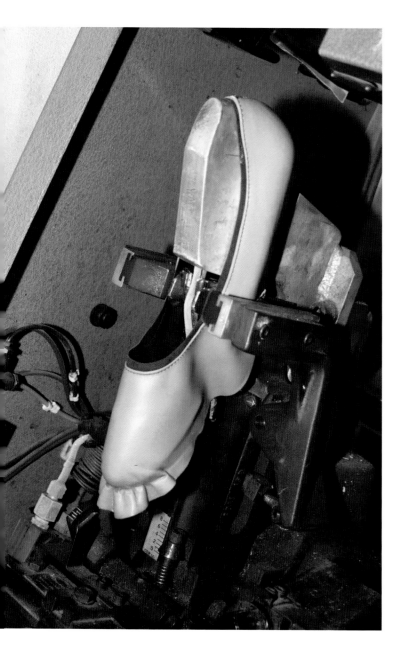

The shaped cover is held tightly in this machine while a metal wedge is pressed into the heel. This is to strengthen and reinforce the heel. The toe of the shoe is similarly reinforced.

Here the cover has been removed from the back part moulding machine. It can be seen that the heel has been hardened and reinforced to retain shape. The pleated area is part of the lasting margin, the narrow folded section that continues around the bottom edge of the cover. This lasting margin is the allowance that is glued to the insole.

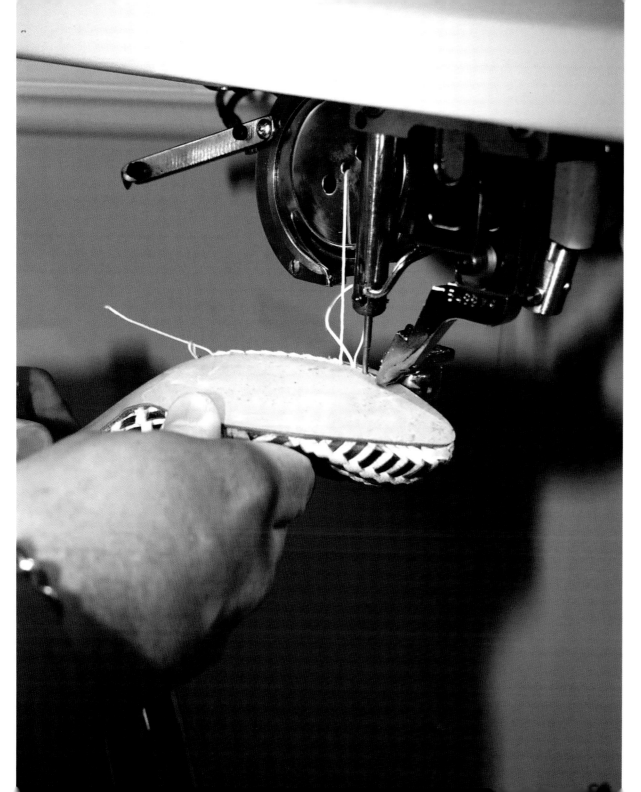

Once the cover has been lasted, that is shaped and glued as described in the previous steps, the sole is prepared and attached. This machine demonstrates a sole being stitched to the lasted cover (although this process is rarely used on a shoe of this type.) This machine has been purchased to encourage the development of design ideas and to give students greater scope in terms of construction techniques. It enables students to learn and consider constructions such as those found in Veltdschoen (desert boots) or welted shoes, and some other designs,

315

The heel is now attached to the shoe. This machine is a sequential nail heel attacher. It uses nails that are driven in at an angle in sequential order. Modern manufacturers still use this although some manufacturers use a steel staple. A sock pad is inserted to protect the foot from the head of the nails or the staples, then an insole lining is cut from a press knife template, or a paper pattern that is measured from the last. The insole lining is fitted into the shoe.

The finished shoe will have its size and the manufacturer's name stamped inside. Rough edges, if any, are smoothed and the cover cleaned or polished in readiness for a sale. The basic steps in making a shoe have been demonstrated, proving it is a slow, careful process. Obviously, decoration and embellishments add more time to the business. And all the machinery and high tech computers have added a new layer of employment to shoemaking—that of mechanics and technicians.

A

Adidas **84-5, 92, 93, 209, 235**
anatomy of a shoe **20**
ankle boots **35, 137, 162, 203, 242**
ankle straps **82, 96, 121, 142, 225**
Astaire, Fred **81**
austerity chic **99**
Azagury, Joseph **266, 270**

B

Baby Dolls **117, 118, 121, 260**
Baby Janes **154, 170, 207, 235**
Baker, Josephine **48, 49, 76**
Balenciaga **286**
ballet pumps **128, 134, 143, 260**
Bally **86, 276-7**
Balmain **286**
Balmoral boots **35**
Bardot, Brigitte **121, 128, 151**
barettes **36, 42**
Bata **89, 108-9, 111**
beadwork **42, 52, 55, 91, 249**
bespoke shoes **40, 43, 55**
Biba **164, 169, 177, 203**
Birkenstocks **168, 188, 196**
Blahnik, Manolo **193, 200, 215, 230-1, 236**
bobby-soxers **124, 125**
boot shoes **265, 266**

boots **15, 34-5, 36, 101, 108, 126, 148, 158, 159, 162-3, 164, 177, 181, 182, 196, 203, 240, 242, 274-5, 288**
brocade **24, 25, 82, 83, 181, 201**
brogues **39, 74, 75, 190**
Bruno Magli **152-3, 170, 185, 213**
buckles **25, 27, 30, 38, 41, 137, 270**
buttoned boots **36, 37**
buttonhooks **37**

C

Cadabra, Theo **306-7**
California casuals **139**
cantilevered shoes **136**
Capezio, Salvatore **134-5**
Cardin, Pierre **148**
Carmen Miranda **86, 111**
Cartier, Roland **197**
Cartland, Barbara **52, 73**
celebrity culture **246, 252, 292**
Chanel **63, 123, 141, 246, 270, 305**
Cher **199, 202**
Choo, Jimmy **236, 238-9, 246, 288, 308**
chopines **21, 23, 305**
Clarks **242, 244-5**
Clergerie, Robert **232, 266, 290-1**
clogs **17, 25, 185, 188**
clothes rationing **97, 107, 111, 118, 121**
cobblers **38**
Colette **63**
Converse **67, 219**

cordwainers **17, 18, 20, 21, 38**
Cordwainers College, London **215, 308-17**
Courreges, André **154, 162**
court shoes **38, 43, 81, 117, 123, 140, 143, 144, 170, 171, 196, 260**
Cox, Patrick **232**
Crocs **257**
Cuban heels **43, 97**

D

dance shoes **44-9, 52, 56-7, 79, 81, 82, 83, 236**
De Havilland, Terry **178-9, 182, 240**
decorative heels **62, 63, 122, 123, 201, 226**
demob shoes **143**
Diana, Princess of Wales **206, 239, 246**
Dior **116-17, 121, 122, 129**
Doc Martens **116, 172, 174, 175, 192-3, 196, 203, 232**

E

Earhart, Amelia **78**
Earth shoes **188**
economic recessions **70, 259**
embroidery **24, 28, 33, 52, 56, 76, 177, 196, 249**
environmentalism **165, 254, 257, 297**
espadrilles **111, 185, 196, 240**

evening shoes **61, 64, 82, 95, 99, 123, 170, 190**
Evins, David **100-1, 111, 123, 163, 305**
evolution of the shoe **12-17**

F

fashion, women's **31, 63, 78, 82, 83, 116, 117, 121, 151, 154, 169, 170, 172, 189, 197, 200, 206, 225, 227, 228**
feminism **176, 189, 191, 196, 197, 199**
Fendi **270**
Ferragamo, Salvatore **61, 79, 86, 89, 90-1, 92, 99, 103, 105, 106, 111, 112, 119, 130, 145, 201, 226**
fetish and bondage footwear **178, 249, 303, 305**
fitness culture **63, 66-7, 70, 113, 137, 207, 208, 279**
see also sports shoes
flip-flops **15, 169, 298**
foot binding **300**
foot measurements **17**
Foster, Joseph **92**

G

galoshes **33, 70**
Garland, Judy **112, 119**
Girls Aloud **272**
'glam rock' **181, 183**
go-go boots **162**
golfing shoes **138, 139**
Greeks and Romans **12, 13, 14**

H

H&R Rayne **62, 89, 107, 121, 122, 123, 129, 151, 166-7, 171, 185, 201**
half-sizes **51, 57**
'health' footwear **188, 196, 235, 257**
Hepburn, Audrey **128**
Herbert Levine Company **126-7, 163, 185**
see also Levine, Beth
high heels **22, 23, 25, 40, 80, 82, 86, 104, 121, 184, 195, 196, 197, 200, 226, 232, 269**
hippies **165, 169, 177, 181**
Hollywood **49, 83, 89, 94, 113, 124, 145, 197**
Hope, Emma **249, 281, 308**
Hulanicki, Barbara **164**

J

jelly shoes **222, 240**
Jerrold, Margaret **137**
Johnson, Amy **79**
Jourdan, Charles **76, 137, 191, 201, 204-5, 215, 232**
Jourdan, Roland **137, 204**
JP Tod **188, 189**

L

lace **128, 130, 142, 197**
laced boots **35, 181**
Lady Gaga **250**
lasts **20, 309**
Lenglen, Suzanne **66**
Levine, Beth **126, 131, 132, 136, 148, 305**

Little, Dave **177**
loafers **154, 169, 188, 232, 237, 305**
Louboutin, Christian **249, 262-3, 270**
Louis heels **30, 64**

M

McCardell, Claire **128, 134**
Madonna **227, 263**
making a shoe **308-17**
Manfield, Moses **55**
Marcos, Imelda **204**
Masai Barefoot Technology (MBT) **235**
Massaro **123, 140-1**
Mayer, Paul **201**
Mazza, Samuel **305**
metal arch supports **79, 91**
Minogue, Kylie **282**
Miu Miu **246**
moccasins **15, 188, 189, 245**
Model, Philippe **215**
Monroe, Marilyn **129, 133**
motor racing **71, 73, 74**
Mugler, Thierry **222**
mules **23, 24, 33, 36, 69, 121, 127, 131, 132-3, 136, 144, 179, 183, 185, 196, 249**

N

New Look **116, 117, 121, 129**
Nice, Hellé **73, 74**
Nike **84, 209, 218-19, 235**
novelty shoes **300-7**

O

overshoes 25, 28
Owens, Jesse 84, 85, 93
oxfords 39, 97, 98, 107, 139, 175, 182, 190, 232

P

Paltrow, Gwyneth 266
pantoufles 24
Parton, Dolly 198, 199, 202
patent leather 61, 130, 156, 194
pattens 28
peep-toes 81, 86, 97, 104, 121, 142, 183, 260, 265, 303
Perugia, André 49, 57, 76-7, 86, 89, 99, 118, 123, 170
Pfister, Andrea 170, 201, 212-13, 221
pikes 18
Pinet, François 40, 55, 64-5
plastics 132, 158, 162, 163, 182, 222, 257, 303
platform shoes 86, 89, 111-13, 141, 176, 178, 180, 181, 182, 183, 236, 272, 286, 288
pointed toes 18, 19
see also winkle pickers
Pollini, Armando 185
power dressing 200, 225
Prada 286
Presley, Elvis 125
pumps 31, 33, 61, 123, 137, 151, 161, 169, 170, 171, 190, 191, 194, 206, 207, 249
see also ballet pumps

punks 172, 175, 203, 207, 303
PVC 158, 182

Q

Quant, Mary 156-8

R

R. Griggs 175, 192-3
Rayne see H&R Rayne
Reebok 84
reptile skins 97, 98, 107, 185
riding boots 240
Rogers, Ginger 81
Rosetti Fratelli 186-7, 188

S

saddle shoes 74
Saint Laurent, Yves 151, 163, 177, 207
Saks Fifth Avenue 113, 114-15
Salamander Company 62, 89
sandal slippers 33
sandals 12-14, 15, 21, 31, 79, 81, 82, 86, 88-9, 99, 100, 104, 138, 139, 148, 184, 190, 196, 221, 242, 269, 270
Second World War 97-106
Sex and the City 236, 239, 263
shoehorns 37
slap shoes 23
slave sandals 270
slingbacks 97, 127, 137, 143, 303

slippers 69, 74
sneakers 66, 109, 113, 124, 125, 137, 138, 281
social change 39, 48, 124, 147, 148, 159, 165, 171
social unrest 30, 149, 172, 194, 254, 257
spats 81
spectator shoes 98, 124, 138, 139, 190
Sperry, Paul 92
sports shoes 39, 40, 66-7, 84-5, 92, 93, 109, 113, 137, 138-9, 209-10, 215, 218-19, 235, 279
Spring-O-Laters 126, 127, 132, 136, 179
squared-off toes 148, 158, 260
Steiger, Walter 160-1
stiletto heels 91, 129, 130, 131, 149, 178, 179, 201, 202, 249, 263, 288
stocking boots 126, 127
suede 95, 97, 99, 112, 116, 125, 128, 188, 190

T

T-bars 46, 64, 74
tennis shoes 66, 113, 137
textile shoes 94, 99, 104, 184
Thatcher, Margaret 199, 200
theatrical footwear 305
trainers 85, 109, 209-10, 218-19, 235, 237, 279
Troy, Seymour 50-1, 57
Turner, Tina 224, 225
turnshoes 17, 18
Twiggy 154, 156, 159

U

Ugg boots 274, 275

V

Velcro 101, 235
Versace, Gianni 227, 228, 249, 270
Vivier, Roger 89, 129, 171
Vivo Barefoot 257
Vogue 44, 67, 94, 95, 97, 99, 123, 194, 225, 242, 282
Vuitton, Louis 288

W

waterproof shoes 39
wedgies 89, 92, 99, 102-6, 111, 113, 118, 119, 131, 185, 216, 221, 236, 240, 305
Weitzman, Stuart 215, 226
Wellington boots 108
welted shoes 18
Westwood, Vivienne 236, 302-3
Williams, Serena and Venus 279
winkle pickers 130, 144, 149

Y

yachting shoes 39
Yantorny, Pietro 56, 58-9

SHOES BIBLIOGRAPHY

The Seductive Shoe, Jonathan Walford, Thames&Hudson 2007

The Biba Collection, Alwyn W Turner, Antique Collectors Club 2004

Fifty Shoes That Changed The World, Design Museum, Conran Octopus 2009

Shoes, Lucy Pratt and Linda Woolley, Victoria and Albert Museum, 1999

Shoes, Linda O'Keefe, Workman Publishing Co 1996

Lifework, Norman Parkinson, Octopus Books 1986

In Vogue, Georgina Howell, Penguin 1975

The Middle Ages, A Concise Encyclopedia Thames&Hudson, 1989

Encyclopedia Britannica

Shoemaking, June Swann, Shire Publications 2003

Vogue (UK) April 1996
Vogue (USA) October 1997
Vogue (UK) September 2009

Websites

eng.shoes-icons.com
Wikipedia
randomhistory.com

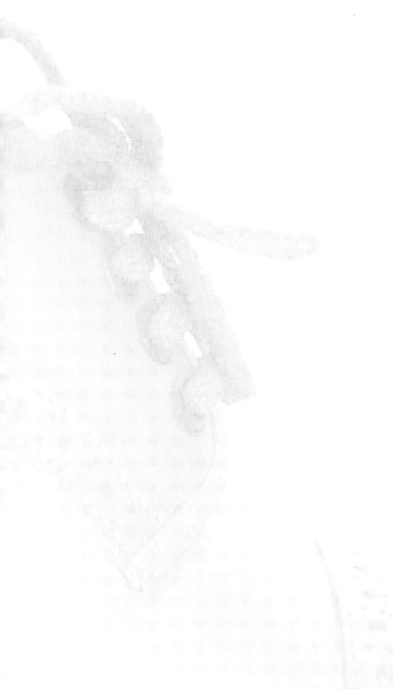

Thanks to the following agencies and people for supplying pictures:
Getty Images, London, England.
Corbis, London, England.
Mirco De Cet Archives, Edgmond, Newport, England.
Bacroom Designs and Advertising - P20 Artwork.
U.S. Library of Congress, Washington DC, USA.
Birkenstock Orthopädie GmbH & Co. KG. Vettelschloss, Germany.
Emma Hope, London, England - Page 278.
Thea Rooke - Page 307.

Special thanks also to the following people and organisations for allowing us to photograph examples from their collections:
Tessa Paul.
The Fashion Museum, Bath, England.
Haley Rose – for digging out a wonderful array of shoes at such short notice.
Northampton Museum and Art Gallery, Northampton, England.
Candy Says, Brentwood, England.   www.candysays.co.uk
Courtesy of Durham University, old Fulling Mill Museum of Archaeology, England – Page: 14-15 and 18.